Middle Management in FE

Ann R. J. Briggs

continuum

Continuum International Publishing Group

The Tower Building
11 York Road
London SE1 7NX

80 Maiden Lane, Suite 704
New York
NY 10038

British Library Cataloguing-in-Publication Data
A catalogue record for this book is available from the British Library.

ISBN: 0-8264-8730-0 (paperback)

Library of Congress Cataloging-in-Publication Data
A catalog record for this book is available from the Library of Congress.

Typeset by YHT Ltd
Printed and bound in England by Antony Rowe Ltd, Chippenham, Wilts.

Middle Management in FE

CITY COLLEGE
NORWICH

Other Titles in the Essential FE Toolkit Series

Books for Lecturers

Teaching the FE Curriculum – Mark Weyers

e-Learning in FE – John Whalley, Theresa Welch and Lee Williamson

FE Lecturer's Survival Guide – Angela Steward

Guide to Diversity and Inclusion in FE – Anne-Marie Wright, Sue Colquhoun, Sina Abdi-Jama, Jane Speare and Tracey Partridge.

How to Manage Stress in FE – Elizabeth Hartney

Guide to Teaching 14–19 – James Ogunleye

Ultimate FE Lecturer's Guide – Ros Clos and Trevor Dawn

A to Z of Teaching in FE – Angela Steward

Getting the Buggers Motivated in FE – Sue Wallace

Books for Managers

Everything You Need to Know About FE Policy – Yvonne Hillier

Middle Management in FE – Ann Briggs

Managing Higher Education in Colleges – Penny Blackie and Anne Thompson

Survival Guide for College Managers and Leaders – David Collins

Senior Leadership and Governance in FE – Adrian Perry

Guide to Financial Management – Julian Gravatt

Guide to Race Equality in FE – Beulah Ainley

Ultimate FE Leadership and Management Handbook – Jill Jameson and Ian McNay

A to Z for every Manager in FE – Susan Wallace and Jonathan Gravells

Guide to VET – Terry Hyland and Chris Winch

Contents

Series foreword

THE ESSENTIAL FE TOOLKIT SERIES
Jill Jameson
Series Editor

In the autumn of 1974, a young woman newly arrived from Africa landed in Devon to embark on a new life in England. Having travelled half way round the world, she still longed for sunny Zimbabwe. Not sure what career to follow, she took a part-time job teaching EFL to Finnish students. Having enjoyed this, she studied thereafter for a PGCE at the University of Nottingham in Ted Wragg's Education Department. After teaching in secondary schools, she returned to university in Cambridge, and, after graduating, took a job in ILEA in 1984 in adult education. She loved it: there was something about adult education that woke her up, made her feel fully alive, newly aware of all the lifelong learning journeys being followed by so many students and staff around her. The adult community centre she worked in was a joyful place for diverse multiethnic communities. Everyone was cared for, including 90-year-olds in wheelchairs, toddlers in the crèche, ESOL refugees, city accountants in business suits, and university-level graphic design students. In her eyes, the centre was an educational ideal, a remarkable place in which, gradually, everyone was helped to learn to be who they wanted to be. This was the Chequer Centre, Finsbury, EC1, the 'red house', as her daughter saw it, toddling in from the crèche. And so began the story of a long interest in further education that was to last for many years . . . why, if they did such good work for so many, were FE centres so under-funded and unrecognized, so underappreciated?

It is with delight that, 32 years after the above story began, I write the Foreword to *The Essential FE Toolkit*, Continuum's new series of 24 books on further education (FE) for teachers and college leaders. The idea behind the *Toolkit* is to provide a

comprehensive guide to FE in a series of compact, readable
books. The suite of 24 individual books are gathered together
to provide the practitioner with an overall FE toolkit in specialist, fact-filled volumes designed to be easily accessible,
written by experts with significant knowledge and experience
in their individual fields. All of the authors have in-depth
understanding of FE. But 'Why is further education important?
Why does it merit a whole series to be written about it?' you
may ask.

At the Association of Colleges Annual Conference in 2005, in
a humorous speech to college principals, John Brennan said that,
whereas in 1995 FE was a 'political backwater', by 2005 it had
become 'mainstream'. John recalled that since 1995 there had
been '36 separate Government or Government-sponsored
reports or white papers specifically devoted to the post-16
sector'. In our recent regional research report (2006) for the
Learning and Skills Development Agency, my co-author
Yvonne Hillier and I noted that it was no longer 'raining policy'
in FE, as we had described earlier (Hillier and Jameson 2003):
there is now a torrent of new initiatives. We thought in 2003
that an umbrella would suffice to protect you. We'd now
recommend buying a boat to navigate these choppy waters, as it
looks as if John Brennan's 'mainstream' FE, combined with a
tidal wave of government policies, will soon lead to a flood of
new interest in the sector, rather than end anytime soon.

There are good reasons for all this government attention on
further education. In 2004/2005, student numbers in LSC-
funded further education increased to 4.2 million, total college
income was around £6.1 billion, and the average college had
an annual turnover of £15 million. Further education has
rapidly increased in national significance regarding the need for
ever greater achievements in UK education and skills training
for millions of learners, providing qualifications and workforce
training to feed a UK national economy hungrily in competition with other OECD nations. The 120 recommendations of
the Foster Review (2005), therefore, in the main encourage
colleges to focus their work on vocational skills, social inclusion
and achieving academic progress. This series is here to consider
all three of these areas and more.

The series is written for teaching practitioners, leaders and managers in the 572 FE/LSC-funded institutions in the UK, including FE colleges, adult education and sixth-form institutions, prison education departments, training and workforce development units, local education authorities, and community agencies. The series is also written for PGCE/Cert Ed/City & Guilds Initial and continuing professional development (CPD) teacher trainees in universities in the UK, USA, Canada, Australia, New Zealand and beyond. It will also be of interest to staff in the 600 Jobcentre Plus providers in the UK and to many private training organizations. All may find this series of use and interest in learning about FE educational practice in the 24 different areas of these specialist books from experts in the field.

Our use of this somewhat fuzzy term 'practitioners' includes staff in the FE/LSC-funded sector who engage in professional practice in governance, leadership, management, teaching, training, financial and administration services, student support services, ICT and MIS technical support, librarianship, learning resources, marketing, research and development, nursery and crèche services, community and business support, transport and estates management. It is also intended to include staff in a host of other FE services including work-related training, catering, outreach and specialist health, diagnostic additional learning support, pastoral and religious support for students. Updating staff in professional practice is critically important at a time of such continuing radical policy-driven change, and we are pleased to contribute to this nationally and internationally.

We are also privileged to have an exceptional range of authors writing for the series. Many of our series authors are renowned for their work in FE, having worked in the sector for 30 years or more. Some have received OBE or CBE honours, professorships, fellowships and awards for contributions they have made to FE. All have demonstrated a commitment to FE that makes their books come alive with a kind of wise guidance for the reader. Sometimes this is tinged with world-weariness, sometimes with sympathy, humour or excitement. Sometimes the books are just plain clever or a fascinating read, to guide practitioners of the future who will read these works. Together, the books make up a considerable portfolio of assets for you to take with you through your journeys in FE. We hope the experience of reading the books will be interesting, instructive and pleasurable and that experience gained from them will last, renewed, for many seasons.

It has been wonderful to work with all of the authors and with Continuum's UK Education Publisher, Alexandra Webster, on this series. The exhilarating opportunity of developing such a comprehensive toolkit of books probably comes once in a lifetime, if at all. I am privileged to have had this rare opportunity, and I thank the publishers, authors and other contributors to the series for making these books come to life with their fantastic contributions to FE.

Dr Jill Jameson
Series Editor
March, 2006

Series Introduction

In his Review of Further Education (FE) published in November, 2005, Sir Andrew Foster described the FE sector as 'the neglected middle child' of UK education provision, to describe its role, sandwiched between the compulsory school sector and higher education. Sir Andrew called for improvements in the image, purpose, leadership and skills focus of the sector. (Foster, 2005). What is there about this idea of 'middleness' that is so important in FE, particularly in 'in-between' roles in management and leadership of the sector? Ann Briggs, Professor of Educational Leadership at the University of Newcastle upon Tyne, explains the role and importance of 'middle' managers in the FE sector in this fascinating and timely book. Ann reflects on the ways in which thousands of FE managers, operating at 'in-between' levels in further education, can and do provide influential, creative, crucially important differences in achieving good quality results for students, staff and management throughout the sector.

Ann has excellent background experience of management and leadership in FE, particularly in analysing the complex roles played by middle managers in a range of different types of jobs. She guides us confidently and sensitively through the labyrinth of difficult issues we need to consider to provide effective management and leadership at middle management level in further education, putting forward a number of formative, unique models for middle management roles in the sector, deriving from original research in FE carried out over several years.

Ann observes in her introduction that if you browse through management and leadership books at a popular bookstall, you will find little or nothing dedicated to managers in colleges, particularly not for those at middle management levels. Here, for the first time, is a book dedicated wholly to middle managers and leaders in FE. This is a crucially important book to guide the sector, drawing on first-hand experience informed by research with 288 middle management team members, 45 middle managers and 16 senior managers in FE, followed by consultancy and staff development activities involving 100 middle managers from a range of different colleges. Ann provides an analysis of the national occupational standards for management and leadership, discussing these standards in her analysis of the roles of FE curriculum managers, managers of services to students and managers of college services, including heads of department, heads of service, and a number of other roles.

Ann feels it is vital that middle managers do not feel like 'victims' trapped in the 'in-between' layers of FE management. She encourages staff working in challenging jobs in middle management to become creative, influential 'new professionals', operating with a unique and empowered voice in the FE sector. Ann provides 'reality checks' to identify and analyse the real-life needs and situations affecting middle managers, including staff development requirements to avoid becoming a hard-pressed victim with a 'piggy in the middle' role. Ann guides us towards recognition of the importance of shared professionalism in ensuring that the role of the FE middle manager is strong and effective throughout the sector. This is an outstandingly useful book for middle managers and leaders, senior management, teachers, tutors and trainers in further education. It will be essential reading on middle management in FE for a long time to come, and I thoroughly commend it to you.

Dr Jill Jameson   *Address and contact:*
Director of Research
School of Education and Training   Mansion House site
University of Greenwich   Bexley Road, Eltham, Greenwich
j.jameson@gre.ac.uk   London SE9 2UG
                                          j.jameson@gre.ac.uk
PhD, MA (King's College, London),   Tel. 02083318058/9502
MA (Goldsmith's), MA (Cantab.),   Fax. 02083319509
PGCE (Nottingham)   P.A. Shirley 02083318058

Introduction

This book is both for and about middle managers in further education (FE) – those who manage curriculum provision, services to students and college services in any post-compulsory college. Why is it needed? If we browse at any railway station or airport bookstall, we will find dozens of books which offer insight and advice about management. We can learn, for example, how to manage our 'boss', how to manage time and stress, how to be 'highly effective'. Help is available by the shelf-load, written by highly acclaimed authors. So why should I write, or you read, this book?

Look again at that airport bookstall, and take your search further, to the shelf in your municipal or academic library. How much insight and advice do you find about being a middle manager in an FE college? How many books do you even see with 'further education' in the title? In the Learning and Skills sector, we are good at adapting. So we adapt advice from books about business management, and gain insight from research into school leadership, and we read the government policy documents about lifelong learning and the Learning and Skills Council (LSC) circulars about funding for post-compulsory education, and we learn to manage.

Unlike some of the bookstall texts, this book will not 'give you the answers'. As far as I know, there are no ten essential tips for managing in a college. All colleges are different; all management jobs are different; most managers' jobs differ from day to day. What this book offers is a number of ways of looking at the middle-manager role in order to make sense of it. Each chapter looks at the role in a different way, and offers tools – diagrams, checklists, questions – to enable readers to apply the insight from the chapter to their own situation. So, step by step, the book enables you to think through aspects of management as they relate to roles in your own college.

This book is based on first-hand experience and on research which has drawn extensively upon others' first-hand experience. 'Managing in the middle' in a number of roles at large and small colleges gave me insight into the nature of college management and the different ways in which colleagues and I undertook our work. When I decided to undertake research into middle management, these experiences enabled me to ask questions for my research: what, generically, do FE middle managers do? What helps them in their role? What impedes them? What insights can we gain from research about how colleges could be better managed? In the course of undertaking the research, I made case study visits to four English FE colleges, interviewing and observing a range of middle managers, their senior managers and teams. The 45 middle managers interviewed had responsibility for college services (for example, finance, estates, management information systems), for services to students (for example, learning resources, learning support, student services) and for curriculum (for example, heads of department, key skills coordinators, curriculum project managers). They were interviewed in groups so that they could share and develop each other's responses to the research questions. Two hundred and eighty-eight of their team members responded to questionnaires about middle management, and 16 senior managers, including the four college principals, gave individual interviews about their perspective on the middle–manager role.

During the process of analysing and writing up the investigation, I presented papers at a number of conferences attended by FE senior and middle managers and people undertaking research into FE leadership and management; I also undertook consultancy and staff development with over 100 middle managers in different colleges. These activities enabled the emerging ideas to be tested, questioned and discussed by fellow researchers and FE professionals. The thinking presented in this book is therefore built on the first-hand experiences of hundreds of FE personnel. This is, admittedly, a small proportion of those employed in FE colleges, but the collective experience represented here is substantial.

This data collection was undertaken in 2001; the analysis was completed in 2003. Since then, all four case study colleges have new principals, and the full impact of the move to LSC funding has had effect. Key government reports have been issued, such as *Realising the Potential* (Foster 2005), and the 14–19 initiative launched by *Success for All* (DfES 2002) has taken effect. So why are these experiences relevant now, when the sector is so constantly changing? They are important because, through talking about their lives as managers in 2001, the respondents were saying things about the middle management role which are valid beyond changes in policy, principalship or funding regime. They were offering insights into ways in which managers operate in large, unwieldy organizations which nevertheless have strong society-based values, and a deep commitment to students and their learning. The managers showed how an awareness of whole-college issues is needed, even when managing a small department. They demonstrated the extent of their accountability for 'making things happen' in their area of college, and the skills needed to manage the teams who provide learning and support services for students. They illustrated the network of liaison which is necessary to support a programme of learning or an aspect of college services. They manifested their leadership skills through the ways in which they spoke about their teams and the work of their departments – although they were reluctant to be called leaders. They demonstrated the 'juggling' which is necessary to reconcile college-wide systems with individual departmental and student needs. They were acutely aware of their own shortcomings, and those of their college systems.

This book is therefore based upon their collective thinking, together with the observations of those who commented on the research. The voices of the managers, their team members and senior colleagues will be heard as we tease out the issues facing college managers today. Their observations in 2001 will enable us to understand college management in 2010 and beyond.

Throughout the book, you will find 'Reality check' sections where readers who are middle managers can consider their own role. There are a number of diagrams and models which offer ways of thinking about the middle-manager role within its college context, together with suggestions about the ways in which the models may be used to develop the work of managers. There are also sections 'Linking to the occupational standards', which suggest further activities to develop the middle-manager role. All of these activities can form the basis of personal reflection and self-evaluation; they can also be used for formal programmes of staff development. The book is intended for active use in shaping the work of college managers, and improving the context within which they undertake their roles.

1 The middle management context

National context

The learning and skills sector is the largest of the educational sectors in England, with around seven million learners engaged in further education, work-based learning and adult and community education. Within this sector are over 400 colleges including general FE and tertiary colleges, sixth-form colleges, adult education colleges; agriculture and horticulture colleges; art, design and performing arts colleges; and a number of 'specialist designated' colleges. Some colleges, such as land-based colleges and those offering education for people with disabilities, are residential; the majority are not. The number of colleges fluctuates from year to year, mainly as a result of mergers and other local patterns of reorganization. Collectively, they offer full- and part-time courses from basic to postgraduate level to students aged 14 upwards. Around two-thirds of college students are adults in part-time education and training; colleges also provide around 27 per cent of 16–18 year olds in England with full-time education and training, compared with around 22 per cent of this age group who study in schools (data from LSC 2002). FE colleges thus play a very significant part in the educational life of the country.

Colleges within the learning and skills sector have been affected by extensive recent change: each separate influence upon them potentially affects the way they are to be managed. The incorporation of maintained colleges which took effect in 1993 altered their system of governance and made them independent of Local Education Authority (LEA) control. Incorporation entailed the transfer of functions such as finance, estates and human resource management, formerly carried out by the LEAs, to management within colleges. Many colleges responded to this situation by appointing curriculum managers to roles in college services: for example, making them responsible for personnel or building management functions alongside their teaching duties. As the decade progressed, these roles largely became professionalized, and separated from the management of curriculum.

Over the same period, colleges restructured their management systems in response to changes in external funding and accountability regimes, firstly under the Further Education Funding Council (FEFC), and later in 2001 when the LSC took over the responsibility for post-compulsory education other than higher education. One key 'new role' in the post-incorporation college structures has been the management of college information systems. Data systems for reporting to funding bodies have to be aligned to reporting systems within the college which touch on every aspect of the college's work. The complexity of this operation, and the difficulty of meshing effectively the external and internal reporting systems, has been a major source of perceptions of management bureaucracy within colleges.

The new systems for funding post-compulsory education, which included the convergence of college funding systems in the 1990s, meant reduced funding for many colleges, and were a cause of considerable stress in the sector. In the period 1993–7, more than 50 per cent of colleges were reported by the FEFC to be financially insolvent (Gleeson 2001). College management structures were redesigned to fit the available resources. 'Top-heavy', resource-hungry management structures were questioned; colleges were forced to 'shed' staff at all levels through redundancy, early retirement and non-replacement. Staff who remained were rearranged into leaner, tighter systems. Cost efficiency became a major factor in decisions over course provision.

This response to reduced funding was replicated on a larger scale through college amalgamations, in which both market and financial pressures led to the rationalization of provision across urban areas, reducing the number of individual colleges. Since 2000, the funding levels for post-compulsory education have improved. However, the mechanism for funding allocation, and its link with government priorities which may not be aligned with local need, produces problems. For example, at the time of writing (early 2006), there is widespread concern about colleges' ability to offer significant areas of adult learning provision in the coming academic year, due to the current government focus upon educational provision for those aged 14–19. There is also considerable concern in the sector over the lack of parity in funding between schools and colleges.

Changes in the statutory inspection regimes have also had an influence on the management of colleges. Systems of internal self-assessment and external inspection were established, firstly by the FEFC in 1997, later through the Common Inspection Framework operated by the Office for Standards in Education (Ofsted) and the Adult Learning Inspectorate (ALI) from 2001, and by an amalgamation of inspection services from 2006. Each new framework for inspection, and the performance indicators by which colleges are to be assessed, has influenced the structure and operation of college management. External accountability, for example for the quality of discrete areas of curriculum provision or for the management of support for students, has been replicated in the patterns of internal responsibility for those same areas.

Thus, as colleges responded to the changes in external funding, responsibility and accountability, they restructured internally; systems were re-formed and new management roles were designed. In 2001, Lumby reported that of the 164 colleges she surveyed, 160 had restructured between 1993 and 1999, and the majority had restructured more than once: ten per cent had restructured over three times in six years. Since changes to both funding and inspection in 2001, colleges have restructured further, continuing the turbulent conditions for management experienced in the 1990s.

Local context

While the radical changes experienced in the years since incorporation have exerted extensive common pressures upon all post-compulsory colleges, and have induced similar types of

change in their management systems, the management structures within individual colleges remain as diverse as the sector
itself. Local management for colleges, as for schools and universities, leaves each college free to determine how its human
and financial resources are best to be deployed. The internal
management structure of each college, and the college context
within which managers operate, is therefore significantly
dependent upon local circumstance.

One key influence is college size. The largest general FE
colleges have around 25,000 full- and part-time students, and
operate on a number of sites across a city or a region. The
influence of size on management structures may be compounded by geographical location. When colleges operate on
many sites, some middle-management roles are replicated at
each major site, and some managers may operate across a
number of sites. Many colleges also offer teaching in small
outreach centres such as local libraries and schools, where
responsibility for provision may be shared among managers in
combination with other responsibilities. The combination of
size of operation and multiplicity and distance of location offers
logistical problems of communication and liaison between
managers, and the need to maintain the same standards and
procedures across a diverse organization.

A further factor affecting management structure is the range
of subjects and types of programme offered. For example, a
sixth-form college offering predominantly full-time academic
programmes requires a different management structure from
that of a large general FE college which may offer courses in all
the programme areas funded by the LSC, together with a
substantial community education, higher education and full-
cost business training programme. Colleges may operate on
multiple sites across a spectrum of subject provision, aiming to
meet a wide range of academic, vocational and community
needs. Lecturers may meet their students at any time of the day
or evening, on a college site, in the workplace or through
distance-learning links. This presents logistical difficulties for
managers in terms of inter- and intra-departmental liaison,
monitoring the work of staff, keeping in touch with the needs
of stakeholders and meeting with each other to discuss whole-

college issues. Unique management structures are therefore needed to meet the individual needs of each college, and we will consider these structures further in Chapter 2.

Managerialism and the 'New Professionals'

The turbulence produced by the context of change described above created an atmosphere of crisis in the sector, and the development of new college management structures within this turbulent environment resulted in negative attitudes towards managers and management. Colleges were perceived as becoming 'managerial', with a proliferation of managers who made bureaucratic, mechanistic demands on lecturers in order to satisfy the new systems of accountability. There was a difficult political context both surrounding colleges and within them, as a government-induced thrust for efficiency took hold. Elliott (2000) writes of the necessity to increase student enrolment, retention and achievement within a climate of industrial dispute over contracts and insensitive management strategies. Longhurst (1996) sums up the dominant preoccupation of college senior managers as one of maximizing income and minimizing costs, perhaps understandable at a time when more than 50 per cent of colleges were reported to be financially insolvent. Alongside this drive for operational efficiency was a parallel campaign for effectiveness, stimulated both by government requirements in the form of targets, and by a professional concern for educational standards and values. As Lumby (2001, p. 43) observes, achieving the 'twin objectives' of reducing unit costs and increasing efficiency on the one hand, and maintaining the quality of education and the focus on learning on the other, was a central concern for college managers.

This combination of stresses, exacerbated by the industrial disputes, led to perceptions that there were 'oppositional cultures' between lecturers and management (Lumby and Tomlinson 2000, p. 139). Lumby (2001, p. 4) comments that in this period 'lecturers are often portrayed as keeping alight the flame of educational and professional values in the face of oppression by the new strain of manager'. Randle and Brady in 1997 saw managerialism in colleges as being based upon concepts of business efficiency and market demand, and professionalism taking as its basis a concern for professional autonomy and the primacy of the needs of students, and depicted these two stances as irreconcilable. Learning could not be seen as a business. Their views represent contemporary perceptions from the mid-1990s: from the viewpoint of the early 2000s, however, the perspective changes.

The external turbulence continues, but the paradox of the 'business of learning' (Ainley and Bailey 1997) is starting to be reconciled. Over the period since 1993, colleges have learned to be more businesslike, and their business is learning. There are now government-initiated National Occupational Standards for leadership and management in the post-compulsory learning and skills sector (Lifelong Learning UK 2005), which will be discussed later in this chapter. There is a Centre for Excellence in Leadership, founded in 2003, which focuses on the development needs of leaders across the learning and skills sector. Initiatives such as these serve to clarify the purpose and enactment of the 'learning business'.

Accusations of managerialism still persist, and the sector is acknowledged as being overburdened by bureaucracy (Centre for Excellence in Leadership 2005). However, management, rather than being viewed as the rational, mechanistic 'enemy' of professional values, is becoming a more familiar response to the public and market accountability of the sector. Professionalism has moved from being a concept applied retrospectively to some 'golden age' before incorporation, and is also gradually being redefined. What we may call 'New Professionalism' depends upon employees' understanding of the educational values of the institution within its new context of operation, and a response to the professional and cultural accountability of the college. It also depends on the recognition of the concepts of professionalism offered by the service departments of the college, and an adaptation to the necessary aspects of managerialism. Simkins and Lumby (2002) propose that managerialism and professionalism represent different understandings of how student needs should be met, and how quality of performance should be measured: in effect, they are different interpretations of accountability. They claim that the values and interests of different groupings of staff can be shared, and that the 'them and us' distinction between senior managers and other staff has become blurred. Similarly, Gleeson and Shain (1999) conclude that professionalism is interpreted differently by different people, but that there are commonly accepted core values upon which a new professionalism can be based. They also note that staff who have joined colleges since incorporation are more accepting of the current context for management.

The evidence and understanding presented in this book contribute to the debate about manager professionalism. We shall therefore return to the issue in Chapter 9 in order to define professionalism more clearly within the context of this book.

National standards for management

Throughout the late 1990s, the Further Education National Training Organisation (FENTO) collaborated throughout the UK with managers in the sector, their employers and related organizations to produce the National Occupational Standards for Management in Further Education. Early drafts of the standards – commonly known as the FENTO standards – were widely discussed, and they were trialed in 12 UK colleges before their eventual publication in 2001. They were later revised and reissued as the National Occupational Standards for leadership and management in the post-compulsory learning and skills sector in 2005 (Lifelong Learning UK 2005).

The opening sections of the standards give a brief overview of the nature of FE management, the values and assumptions upon which the standards are based, and the generic knowledge, understanding and attributes needed to undertake the role. The key areas of management are then introduced, with the understanding that the nature of the management within these areas differs at first-line manager level, middle- and senior-management level. The key areas and their purposes are:

A   Develop strategic practice
To analyse, plan, develop and implement a shared vision
A1   Develop a vision
A2   Plan to achieve the vision
A3   Manage change and continuous improvement

B   Develop and sustain learning and the learning environment
To plan, implement and review the quality and range of services to promote positive outcomes and success
B1   Develop and sustain services for learners
B2   Manage quality in the delivery of services
B3   Manage human resources to support the provision of services

C   Lead teams and individuals
To lead teams and individuals to enable them to achieve objectives and continually improve performance
C1   Manage and develop self and own performance
C2   Maintain and develop team and individual performance
C3   Build and maintain productive working relationships

D   Manage finance and resources
To manage the acquisition, deployment and development of resources to facilitate and promote learning
D1   Plan resource requirements
D2   Manage finance
D3   Manage physical resources

The main functions of the standards are to offer a competency-based means of self-evaluation, needs identification and formal assessment, and to act as a tool for recruitment and selection and manager development. Competencies are presented at the three different levels of management for each standard.

The standards have proved useful for these purposes, and both formal assessment schemes and staff development programmes have been built upon them. They will be referred to in each of the central chapters of this book, to show how they relate to the ideas presented here. However, the main focus of this book is on understanding the middle-manager role in FE colleges, rather than on assessment of manager performance. The findings from the research in colleges which underpin the book enable us to identify what middle managers do, and which key issues affect their role; these insights offer a valuable context within which to apply the standards. The next chapter moves on to discuss the range of roles which middle managers occupy, and the college structures within which they work.

2 Who are the middle managers?

The range of middle-management roles within any one college is considerable, both in its breadth and depth. Areas of management responsibility 'across' the college range from managing catering facilities and student counselling to managing the college's higher education provision and outreach programmes in the community. In any one of these areas there are 'layers' of management, from managers who work closely with the senior team of the college to first line managers responsible for a discrete curriculum area or college service team. This middle section of the management structure includes a number of the 'new' management roles transferred to colleges at incorporation, or developed since that time, together with the longer established curriculum management roles. In this book, we will consider the roles within three broad groupings:

- curriculum managers, responsible for subject or programme areas
- managers of services to students, such as learning resources, learning support or student services
- managers of college services, such as estates, finance or personnel.

The purpose of any middle management role is to transform strategic policy into strategic practice. Middle managers may not be included on a regular basis in whole-college decision-making and policy formation, yet they are instrumental in ensuring that the decisions and policies made are carried out by their teams. The nature of their role means that they may also have considerable 'local' knowledge, power and autonomy; they may be responsible for large areas of curriculum provision, or for key departments within the college. Management structures which enable middle managers to work effectively are crucial to the effectiveness of the whole college, since they are the ones who, in Bennett's terms (1995, p. 18) 'articulate the vision': on a day-to-day basis they make the business of the college happen. This is a difficult, intriguing and rewarding role, and to understand it better we need first to consider how college management structures operate.

Management structures

Given the diversity of the sector, and its constant state of change, any representation of management systems across the sector is only approximate. For simplicity of presentation, a generic management structure is offered here as Figures 1 and 2. FE colleges operate on a day-to-day basis through a senior management team (SMT), who, under the overall authority of the college governors, are accountable for the management of the college. This team is led by a person who may be named Principal, Chief Executive or Director; the size, name and composition of the team varies, but usually includes senior managers responsible for curriculum and college services.

At the base of the hierarchical structure are manual workers, administrators and lecturers who have responsibility for no-one but themselves, although their job involves liaison and cooperation with others. Between the apex and base of the triangle there are usually several 'layers' of management and responsibility. For college service functions, such as finance and estates, and for services to students, such as learning support or student services, the pattern might be as depicted in Figure 1.

Where managing the curriculum is concerned, there are greater numbers of departments and staff involved, and management 'lines' may therefore be longer; the roles might be as represented in Figure 2.

In each college, the naming and the number of the 'layers' varies; curriculum directors may also operate as heads of faculty, and there may be further 'director' role-holders to whom middle managers must answer – for example, directors of quality, resources or external relations.

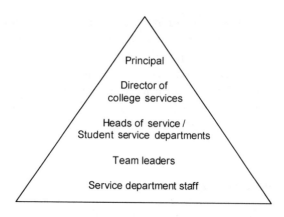

Figure 1 Hierarchy of roles for college services and student services

Figure 2 Hierarchy of roles for curriculum provision

By constructing two 'triangles,' we have already replicated one problem which college middle managers face. A curriculum manager may be placed within a line of responsibility which has near the top a deputy or vice principal who is responsible for curriculum. A manager of a college service or a service to students may operate in a totally different 'line', ultimately answerable to a different deputy. Seen from the top of the organization, this pattern makes sense: it offers clear lines of specialist responsibility. But consider college provision from the student perspective. Students, who are the responsibility of a particular curriculum manager, are admitted to the college by means of the marketing and student services departments, occupy classrooms supplied and maintained by the estates department, and are taught by lecturers who are employed through the human resources department, managed by the curriculum manager and evaluated by systems set up by the quality office. Their registration, attendance and achievements are tracked and reported to the funding agencies and to the college finance office by the college management information service. They register for their examinations through an examinations office, and may receive funding for childcare or maintenance through the finance department. They make use of learning resources, information technology services and learning support services supplied by three further departments, and may receive careers or personal counselling through student services.

From the student perspective, those clear lines of responsibility are invisible, perhaps irrelevant. What the student needs is a complex web of provision which weaves across all the lines, constructed and maintained to meet their needs. In a large organization, such a web is difficult to conceive, build and operate; in practice, managers attempt to construct it on an individual basis, without it being a visible and acknowledged college structure. So a system designed for line management creaks and flexes as individual managers try to apply it to another purpose: the provision of learning for students. In the simpler systems in operation before incorporation, the roles we are considering were closer together, mainly held by staff with combined responsibility for curriculum and another area of college provision. We have been witnessing some kind of 'continental drift' as the constituent parts of college management potentially drift further and further apart. What will bring managers together is a better understanding of the roles that they collectively and individually undertake.

Let us consider again the list of responsibilities set out in the leadership and management standards (Lifelong Learning UK 2005):

- Develop strategic practice.
- Develop and sustain learning and the learning environment.
- Lead teams and individuals.
- Manage finance and resources.

All managers perform these activities to some extent in their role. At the very least, they are expected to have a general competence in understanding and carrying out the function of, say, leading teams or managing resources. At the same time, a key activity from the list is the main focus of the role: the manager may be in charge of a curriculum area, IT provision for students or college finance. If the web of provision envisaged above is working effectively, managers who have only a general knowledge of, say, teaching or providing student support would consult the college experts in these areas in order to develop their own expertise and improve their area of provision. What tends to happen in practice is that the college structures and systems stand in the way of such liaison and organizational learning: managers work within their own 'boxes', unaware of, or untrusting of, the expertise of others.

The organizational theorist Mintzberg (1990, p. 166) claims that managers generally work intuitively: 'The strategic data bank of the organisation is not in the memory of its computers but in the minds of its managers.' The intuitive nature of the work of educational managers is highlighted by Bennett (1995), writing in a schools context, where he proposes that middle managers make decisions based upon their individual 'assumptive world'. The assumptive world of each manager is unique; it is based on personal values and on the manager's analysis of previous experience. If each middle manager in our web of provision is acting intuitively, basing their actions on their previous experience, with no agreed clarity over how their roles should interact, the chances of effective provision for learners are greatly reduced.

Another problem presents itself at this point. Research into organizations is a useful basis upon which to construct first theory, and then new practice. The management of FE colleges has been little researched, and middle manager research in educational settings has largely focused upon the curriculum manager role. We have seen that college managers in a wide range of roles occupy the pivotal position of translating policy into practice: to consider college middle management as a coherent whole, all roles must be considered, not simply those most directly linked with teaching and learning.

Reality check

You are probably not in a position to restructure your college, and restructuring is generally a painful process, instinctively to be avoided. However, take some time to consider the management structures of your college, in order to understand your own role better.

- How does your college represent its management structures?
- Does it actually operate in this way?
- How do the structures help you to play your part in providing effective learning experiences for students?
- How do they hinder you?
- If, in fact, you are operating in a personally adapted version of the official structure, what are your adaptations designed to achieve? Do they help you to play your part in providing effective learning experiences for students? Do they help or hinder other managers?
- Could these adaptations be more widely used to enable coherent practice across the college?

Managing in the 'buffer zone'

Read any book about middle management, and you will recognize the experience of managing in the 'buffer zone', in which managers attempt to absorb the impact of demands from both the senior managers and their teams and to mediate between them. Read the research literature on middle management in FE, and you will find the same picture. Consider the 'basic' work of the manager – implementing strategy, carrying out activities to develop and support learning, managing and leading teams of staff, managing resources – and the role of liaison emerges as important, particularly in the form of translation and brokering activities. From their research in English FE colleges, Gleeson and Shain (1999, pp. 461–2) see academic middle managers as 'mediators of change'. They 'filter change in both directions', 'translating policy into practice in ways which are acceptable and make sense to both groups [i.e. senior managers and team members]' (Gleeson and Shain 1999, pp. 470–1). In doing so, they are, according to Gleeson and Shain, 'constructing the art of the possible'. This activity demands liaison skills, interpersonal skills and a keen appreciation of the professional needs and value base of the people concerned.

Adopting a 'buffer role' can present problems for both the manager and the team. The instinct to protect or exclude one's team from college-wide concerns is strong, particularly when their workload is heavy, but it can result in team members becoming isolated from the strategic purpose of the college, and having an unrealistic picture of their own role. Paternalistic and maternalistic approaches to leadership, which respectively exclude and protect staff from whole-college concerns, are discussed by Drodge (2002) and Leathwood (2000), in their researches into FE management. These writers consider that exclusive and protective approaches can disempower team members, as they may be prevented from understanding their working context clearly, and may become over-dependent upon the manager.

The function of buffers is to absorb impact, and Alexiadou (2001, pp. 417) considers that responsive middle managers are willing to absorb much of the impact of change, and to generate structures which accommodate new realities. She writes of FE managers' decisions being made within the range of what is 'affordable', based upon educational values, concern for community and collegiality. Gillett-Karam (1999, pp. 5–6), reporting on US community colleges, makes very similar observations: that mid-level managers are 'the buffer between faculty and administration' – that is, between teaching staff and senior management – and that they act as conduits, mediators, communicators and facilitators. She comments that 'leading from the middle is no easy task'.

This task can involve not only leading in the middle of the institution, but also leading from the middle of a team. Being part of the team involves managers in a 'dual role' of both teaching and managing, or managing a service while carrying out its basic operations. This is generally acknowledged to put pressure on the manager, limiting the time available for management; Lumby (1997, p. 350) considers that in colleges the dual role has encouraged an 'amateur approach to management' which is no longer applicable. Conversely, some managers wish to retain the dual role, as it keeps them in touch with the essential purpose of their management activity, whether this is teaching, supporting students or operating a college service.

Being part of the team also subjects the manager to powerful influence from colleagues within their departments. Pritchard (2000, p. 151) writes about middle managers in FE having difficulty in line-managing people with whom they have worked on an equal basis, and having difficulty in implementing what they saw as 'surveillance and enforcement practices'. From research in schools, Tranter (2000, p. 24) puts the subject leader's dilemma into focus: 'Some have seen themselves as the "first among equals" but are now being required to act as line managers.' In a higher education context, Smith (1996, 2002) points out the tensions inherent in being both an academic leader and a line manager. He notes (2002) that staffing issues are deemed the most difficult things an academic head of department has to deal with, a point underlined by Bolton (2000, p. 62), also in a higher education context: 'What do you do with difficult staff? This is one of the most contentious issues which a new Head of Department will have to face.'

Reality check

Represented in Figure 3 are some of the dilemmas involved in managing in the middle: the positions at either end of each spectrum indicate difficult choices to be made in carrying out this role. For example, should you set yourself up as a leader for your team, or try to lead 'as an equal' from within the team? Is

Figure 3 Managing in the middle

it better to protect team members from pressures from within the college, or empower them to understand the complexities of their college context? In these cases, it is difficult to reconcile the choices: the positions at the end of the spectra are not compatible with each other. The dilemmas represented on other spectra may be easier to reconcile: for example, you may translate the needs of senior managers to your team as well as translating team need to senior managers. Here, a preferred stance might be in the middle of the spectrum, 'balancing' the negotiation needs of team members and senior managers.

Middle managers may, however, attempt to adopt stances which are not compatible or consistent with each other, or may adopt uncomfortable compromise positions. Take a little time to think through what each of the spectra represents in your situation. Which line represents your most difficult dilemma, and how could you try to resolve it? On the whole, managers who adopt stances towards the left-hand end of the spectra more overtly accept and enact their leadership and management roles; those acting nearer to the right-hand end follow a philosophy of leading from within the team, and protecting other team members. One strategy to resolve your management dilemma would be to move further to the left or the right, either in your overall approach to management, or in that particular situation. If you do, you need to think through what your new stance implies about the way you carry out your management role.

Expectations upon middle managers

We use the word 'role' very readily, almost without thinking what the term implies. Yet, examining what our role is, is the key to understanding and carrying it out. A role may be seen as a 'defined social position' (Jackson 1972, p. 3), in which the role-holder is the subject of the expectations of others and themselves. A brief look at role theory will enable us to examine the effect of changing, or ambiguous expectations, as well as the effect of overload produced by an excess of expectation.

We might say that a person occupies a position, but performs a role (Burnham 1969). So the role is the set of activities associated with that position, the sum of the expectations upon the role-holder. The role is defined by the *role set*, which comprises all those who have a stake in the performance of the role (Katz and Kahn 1966). The role set can include anyone inside or outside the organization who is connected with the role-holder's behaviour and, importantly, it includes the role-holder. All the members of the role set develop beliefs about what the role-holder should and should not do: collectively they both define and evaluate the person in role (Katz and Kahn 1966). Their expectations, communicated individually and collectively, comprise the *sent role*, and the role-holder's perceptions and understanding of what was sent constitute the *received role* (Kahn et al. 1964, Katz and Kahn 1966).

From these basic definitions, we can identify potential problems. The role is based upon the perceptions, understandings and values of a number of people, including the role-holder, and inevitably there are differences to be reconciled. Members of the role set each have a stake in the role: they need *their* 'version' of the role to be the one which is carried out. This can lead to a number of conflict situations, firstly *role pressure*, in which one or more members of the role set attempts to secure conformity with their expectations. This may become a cause of *role strain*: 'the felt difficulty in fulfilling role obligations' (Goode, 1960, p. 483). Pressure may not come only from one direction; irreconcilable occurrence of two or more role expectations results in *sent role conflict* (Katz and Kahn 1966). In some situations, a single role sender may be inconsistent in their demands upon the role-holder, leading to intra-sender conflict (Kahn *et al.* 1964).

Two further categories of role conflict are important to the middle manager: *role ambiguity* and *role overload*. Under conditions of role ambiguity, the role-holder does not know what to do, either through lack of information, or lack of understanding of how to comply. Some people have a higher tolerance of ambiguity than others; nevertheless, clear and consistent feedback on performance is necessary if the role-holder is to establish a 'meaningful and satisfying self-identity' within the role (Katz and Kahn 1966). Role ambiguity can also occur when there is an imbalance between what role-holders have authority to do, and those activities for which they have responsibility (Hammons 1984). Role overload, as the term suggests, occurs when it is impossible for the person to complete all aspects of the sent roles within the time and with the resources available (Kahn *et al.* 1964).

Anyone who has held a college middle-manager role will recognize most of the situations theorized above. A manager may have a job description which defines the position, but does not define the role: the manager has to work this out for him or herself. On taking up the role, the manager may not know who all the members of the role set are, but may nevertheless be subject to their expectations. The manager's own expectations of the role are likely to conflict with the expectations of others. Pressures build up, as some members of the role set – perhaps senior managers, perhaps key members of the team – try to make the manager perform in certain ways. Ambiguity creeps in: the manager simply does not know what the role comprises, or does not have the authority to perform it all. And inevitably the position of overload is reached: there are too many different things to do, and the manager feels under pressure to do them all.

Reality check

Understanding role theory may not seem to be much help in managing a difficult workload. However, the analysis above can help us to identify what is wrong, and to develop strategies for remedy or for preventative action. If you are experiencing difficulty with your middle-manager role, consider the following questions.

- Who are your role set? How do they tell you what to do? Are their demands clear? Are they reasonable?
- Do you receive conflicting messages about your role from different people, or conflicting messages at different times from the same person? If so, decide what you think it is best to do, and communicate your decision clearly. If necessary, tell people about their conflicting needs of you, and the difficulties which they create.
- Do you give clear messages to your role set as to what you see as your role? How clear do you make the boundaries of your role, to yourself and others? Sometimes it is helpful to retain a little 'fuzziness' around your role, to allow you the scope to develop and adjust it. Your decisions about the extent of the clarity needed will depend upon the culture of your college and the behaviour of other managers.
- Do you simply have too much to do? Why? If you have resolved or prevented some of the issues raised in the questions above, the result should be a more manageable workload.

Managing your role

These first two chapters have mapped out both external and internal contexts for the FE middle-manager role. There are other ways of presenting these contexts – politically, culturally, socially – but portrayed here we have the world in which the middle manager operates. The next five chapters look into the role in more detail, using the research study upon which this book is based as their foundation. The ideas presented in these chapters are based upon the analysis of responses from middle managers, their senior managers and team members to questions about the nature of the middle management role in colleges, and what enables and impedes middle managers in carrying it out. Through the perceptions of the managers and their role sets, five aspects of the middle-manager role have been identified: those of corporate agent, implementer, staff manager, liaison and leader. The following chapters will look at each of these aspects of role in turn. We shall consider what it means to be a college middle manager, how managers undertake their role, and how understanding the role and its working context can enable the manager's work to be carried out more effectively.

3 Managing the college

The work of middle managers is to transform college strategy into action: in effect they manage the operational work of the college. They can therefore be seen as *corporate agents*. The statements below from Colleges A and D, drawn from the research upon which this book is based, illustrate this aspect of the middle manager's role.

> Decisions that get made at a management team level don't actually translate themselves to action unless there are people like us to allocate tasks and oversee them and make it happen. (Curriculum manager, College D)

> They ask the questions and ensure that the college functions. (Student service team member, College A)

Corporate agency depends upon the manager's understanding of how the work of their department relates to the whole work of the college. It involves having knowledge of the 'big picture': having an understanding of whole-college issues, college strategy and the external contexts of the college, and how these relate to their own role. This can be particularly difficult where the college is large, operates on a number of sites or when sections of the college operate independently of each other. Managers who are aware of the values upon which the work of the college is based, and who understand the systems of accountability through which the college operates, will be better able to question, shape and perform the work of the college. Middle managers may have some direct involvement in strategy-making, but their principal role is in adapting and communicating college strategy for action. In the words of the

occupational standards (Lifelong Learning UK 2005), they
'develop strategic practice'.   •

Values, strategy and the 'big picture'

Understanding the 'big picture' involves understanding and
sharing the values on which the purpose of the college is based.
Middle managers in all types of roles demonstrate ways in
which they are guided by their educational values: 'At the end
of the day, it's about knowing the business, it's about knowing
about what makes education tick' (Service manager, College
B). These values underpin many middle-manager activities,
but, in particular, they help the managers' understanding of
their corporate functions. In one college, this understanding
was achieved through the collaborative shaping of the college
values: 'The managers came up with the values of this organization' (Senior manager, College C). In another college, a
senior manager defined the value-base of the whole college as
being support for learning, a perception borne out by middle-
manager responses:

> All of these jobs are still about learning, whether you're 'sites'
> or whether you're 'exams' or 'student services' or 'finance' or
> 'staff services': I think one of the things that is very positive in
> the college is a very strong commitment to ... learning.
> (Senior manager, College B)

> We have got a shared – is the word 'vision'? – with the kind
> of students we deal with and the kinds of experience we
> want them to have and it is pretty solid from the top to the
> bottom ... the students come first. (Curriculum manager,
> College D)

> No matter what we do around this table it's what we give to
> those kids out there and how we bring them on and make
> them better people in society, and that's what it's about.
> (Service manager, College B)

Having a corporate role involves managers in the making and
implementation of strategy. Managers at Colleges A, B and C
reported being involved to some extent in stragegy-making and

all the middle managers surveyed were key players in its implementation. Contributing to strategy involves having regular meetings to discuss it, and networks of departmental and whole-college planning days were in evidence at Colleges B and C. At College A, managers reported being consulted about strategy:

> We feed back into the strategic plan, but we also provide information in that various areas feed into the planning process. (Student service manager, College A)

At College D, strategy was largely 'given' to be implemented and, although managers said that this was done clearly, there was a lack of consistent operational systems to carry it out: 'Six different faculties are all going in different directions' (Service manager, College D). Arguably, cross-college manager discussions about strategy could serve to erode these faculty-based barriers.

Although many middle managers in this research welcomed being part of the strategic planning process, their consensus of opinion is that it is senior managers who devise strategy: 'There is a certain level of consultation, but those objectives are actually set by the senior managers and the governors' (Service manager, College A). Sometimes local strategy, devised by the middle manager, is in conflict with corporate strategy, but, on the whole, the managers' intention is to create a local element of the whole-college picture: 'If there is a policy produced, we try to adhere to it' (Curriculum manager, College B).

The managers' understanding of the 'big picture' is also supported by their awareness of the internal and external contexts of their work, through their liaison activities across the college and externally to it. This gives them an ability, as a Service manager at College A put it, to interpret events at the college on a 'macro' level, and to apply that knowledge within the department. Having a role which demands cross-college networking helps managers to develop an understanding of corporate issues, as it involves them in comprehending and interacting with a range of college agendas. Where the college has a number of sites, management structures are stretched: individual managers who operate on a number of sites may have good corporate understanding, but may be faced with exhausting work schedules. Where their work is limited largely to one of the college sites, college managers' performance in team management is more effective, but they may lack essential knowledge of the whole picture 'across' the sites. Managers occupying service and student service roles feel that they have an advantage here, having a 'wider perspective' (Service manager, College C), and seeing whole-college benefits 'better than the heads of faculty do' (Student service manager, College D). In one of the colleges surveyed, curriculum managers had a number of diverse roles which demanded cross-college interaction; this offered them 'a useful view of the whole college and how it fits together' (Senior manager, College C), and facilitated corporate understanding.

However, the position of 'middleness' means that the managers are not in control of changes in college direction, are often placed in a reactive situation and can sometimes find themselves impeded by being ill-informed. One manager gave the example of working on a project specification, only to find 'that the agenda has changed. It is definitely what *was* wanted, but it isn't where the college is going now' (Service manager, College C).

Middle managers know that, in managing the college, they are subject to external pressures upon the college which influence and alter the nature of their role. The following two managers worked in colleges reacting to turbulent situations, and they spoke about how change within the college affected their corporate role:

> I think it's a difficult position to be in. . . . This organization . . . seems to move extremely quickly, not necessarily in the same direction at the same time, so you have a lot of agendas on the go at once. (Service manager, College C)

> We have to regard ourselves as a business, and we have to be accountable for our funding and so we can't always plan. So if a crisis does come about we have to react and try to solve that crisis. (Student service manager, College B)

The first quotation indicates that the manager is trying to 'keep up' with the college's fast-moving proactive agenda; the second implies a reactive approach by the college to an unforeseen crisis. Both of these corporate scenarios result in instability and confusion for the middle manager, potentially stretching their adaptability beyond its limits.

 ## Reality check

Through thinking about the questions below, you will be able to assess how easy or difficult it is for you to be involved in whole-college issues. As you respond to the questions, think whether there are any negative factors which you could put right yourself, or could improve through negotiation with people who work closely with you. You will have the chance to develop your ideas further through the activities later in the chapter.

- What are the values which underpin your work as a college manager? Do you discuss and share them with your own manager and your team? How do you use them to help you to make decisions?
- How do you gain and develop your understanding of whole-college issues? What college forums or projects could you be involved in, which would improve your understanding, and give you the opportunity to offer your views?
- Does your college operate on a number of sites? If so, how many do you visit regularly? If your college is on a single site, how many other departments or faculties do you liaise with? How easy is it to interact with other middle managers who do different work from you? How well do you understand what they do?
- Do you contribute to whole-college strategy, or is the strategy 'given' for you to carry out? Are there simple ways in which you could improve the balance?
- Think of one way in which college communication could be improved. What could you do to get it implemented?

Accountability

The whole-college function of the middle managers' work involves them in a framework of accountability. The most visible aspects of corporate accountability are those of audit and of conformity to standards. As one senior manager puts it:

> You've got inspection, you're being audited non-stop, there's no choice here, you have to set the standards, you have to monitor the performance. (Senior manager, College A)

She continues: 'But your job as leader – as manager – is to put the human face on it', neatly demonstrating the function of management as an interaction of systems and people, and the balance within the middle-manager role of political and professional accountability (Scott 1989). The middle managers are well aware of their political accountability: the audit role which demonstrates that public funding is being effectively used.

> Some things are checkable, aren't they? It's February – have you got the retention figures? (Curriculum manager, College A)

Middle managers also respond to their market and professional accountabilities – responsibilities to the customer and to education as a profession – through their concern for students, which has a value-driven focus on the learner:

> That's what we are about . . . if we are not getting it right for the students, we should go home. (Student service manager, College A)

As colleges work to rigid bureaucratic structures of external accountability, managers at all levels say that they are helped in their role by internal operational systems which are clear and consistent. Both the clarity and the systems vary between colleges. Of the four colleges surveyed, College A had the longest established and 'tightest' whole-college systems; at College D, the systems were inconsistent between faculties. At the time of the research, College B was in transition from looser value-based systems into clearer frameworks of accountability, while at College C, some systems were secure, but others were in a state of flux following an extensive college merger and the subsequent restructuring activities.

For middle managers, accountability is made more difficult by 'not having full control' (Curriculum manager, College B). One of the senior managers in College B admits: 'We are constantly having to change our own direction ... there hasn't been much consistency.' In his research, Powell (2001) observes that FE middle managers are hampered by poor communication, especially from senior managers, and by a lack of time to respond to new initiatives. As middle managers do not have responsibility for planning whole-college strategy, or for devising shorter-term responses to external pressures, the need here is for effective communication from senior management.

An issue for senior managers is the balance to be struck between empowering middle managers to carry out their role and monitoring their work for compliance to college strategy. As some managers do not 'take ownership of what they should' (Service manager, College C), the monitoring role is necessary. However, monitoring can seem to the middle manager like a lack of trust:

> We are no longer trustworthy, we need to provide proof because otherwise of course we just sit around and smoke cigarettes and talk all day. (Student service manager, College D)

Accountability thus inhabits an uneasy territory between the need for compliance to systems and the issues of manager professionalism, autonomy and trustworthiness.

 ## Reality check

The management of FE is very bureaucratic (see the Annual Report of the Bureaucracy Review Group for Further Education and Training 2004), and accountability can be perceived as a mechanical compliance to systems. How can you 'put a human face' on these systems, for the sake of your team and your students? How can you minimize the bureaucracy and maximize the worth of the audit systems you operate?

Being held accountable can seem like a lack of trust, a disregard for a person's professional motives. It can, conversely, be seen as an acknowledgment that trust is well earned, and a celebration of a person's professional achievement. How can you tip the balance towards the more positive interpretation, for yourself and your team?

Summary

Managers are enabled to be corporate agents through their understanding of whole-college values and through their contribution to whole-college strategy. Knowledge of the 'big picture' enables managers to interpret events which impact upon the college, in order to manage their own situations effectively. Their understanding is aided by cross-college activity. Therefore college structures which encourage networking are beneficial, and managers in student service and service roles, or 'hybrid' roles which involve cross-college liaison, are well placed to gain whole-college understanding. Consistency and clarity of communication and college systems also enable managers to operate effectively at a whole-college level. Managers work within corporate patterns of accountability; this involves creating structures within the department which both 'have a human face', and are coherent with the college as a whole.

Managers may be impeded in their corporate role by their position in the middle of the college structure. They may be located within one section of the college, which prevents them from seeing the whole picture and thinking holistically. They may have little understanding of college strategy, perhaps as a result of having had strategy imposed upon them. Poor communication within the college, and the lack of time to absorb and apply communication strategies, impedes the managers' capacity to grasp whole-college issues. The managers' perception of their accountability within the college system is critical: they may be reluctant to accept the need to comply with audit and monitoring systems, and may feel that accountability erodes their need to be treated as professional, autonomous and trustworthy.

Modelling corporate agency

These issues are summarized in Figure 4: 'Modelling corporate agency'. This is the first of a set of five models which distil key issues affecting the manager role, so that we can explore them further. The research upon which this book is based identified the main features of the college environment which affect the middle-manager role. These are placed in the centre of the model and are linked to the factors which facilitate and impede the middle managers in this aspect of their role. Key factors supporting corporate agency can thus be identified by looking

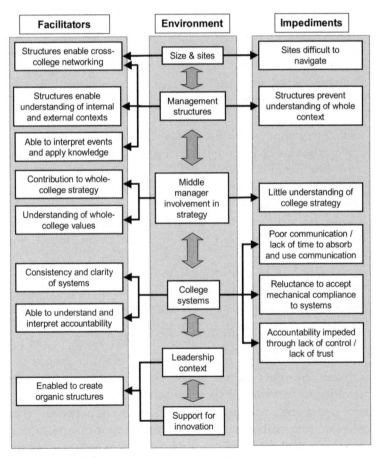

Figure 4 Modelling corporate agency

at the left hand column: they include the clarity and 'usability' of college structures and systems. Factors which enable understanding – of strategy, of accountability, of college values – are also important, as are mechanisms whereby the manager is able to interpret corporate understanding and apply it in their departmental context.

The model may also be read sequentially. If we wish to consider impediments to corporate agency, the following pattern of cause and effect can be constructed, through reading the right-hand side of the model.

If college sites are difficult to navigate, and the structures prevent understanding of the whole-college context, managers have little understanding of whole-college strategy. This lack of understanding, combined with poor communication, may lead to managers' reluctance to comply with mechanical systems, and a lack of acceptance of their corporate accountability.

These readings of the model can help us to identify where problems are located through looking at the clusters where they occur. For example, at College D, one of the senior managers spoke of the middle managers' poor compliance with mechanical procedures. The model enables senior managers to consider how the middle managers' understanding of whole-college accountability and purpose might be improved, and whether the current systems are failing through poor communication, lack of control or lack of trust.

The model can thus be used to understand the context of key features of corporate agency. To take another example, middle managers may be unable to interpret key college events and apply their knowledge appropriately. In other words, one of the facilitators (the third from the top) is missing. To investigate this problem, the other factors in the same cluster could first be examined to see whether they can be strengthened, or whether there is a strong impediment which needs to be addressed. The 'solution' may in fact lie elsewhere in the model – perhaps in the managers' understanding of whole-college values – but the model offers a digest of the complexity of the college environment, which we can scan in order to identify areas for development and action.

Using the model

Try using the model to address the problem of managing on multiple college sites.

As is the case at College C, compensating facilitators can be brought more strongly into play. At this college, management structures are being used to facilitate cross-college networking: the managers' understanding of internal college contexts is developed through the cross-college roles which they have. This does not physically enable access, but it may help the manager to make better use of the access which they have.

At some colleges, middle managers lack understanding of whole-college strategy. It may be inappropriate or logistically difficult to include them more strongly in the strategic planning process. The model suggests that the situation might be improved through finding ways of strengthening managers' understanding of whole-college values and purpose: this would enable them better to understand and apply the 'given' strategy.

The examples offered here demonstrate that the models in this book have two purposes. They simplify and clarify the complexity of the college system, to enable us to understand the factors which impact upon an important part of the managers' role – in this case their role as corporate agent. They also invite us to explore further using the context of our own college, to understand how key factors interact and to conduct problem-solving.

Individual clusters, or sets of facilitators or impediments, can be used as a basis for individual or group-based staff development. The questions offered earlier in the 'reality check' sections can be used to support this activity. The section below helps us to link the issues raised in this chapter to the Occupational Standards for middle managers (Lifelong Learning UK 2005).

Linking to the occupational standards

The issues underpinning corporate agency are closely linked to Key Area A of the occupational standards for middle managers: 'Develop strategic practice'. The standards for Key Area A contain the following sub-sets of activities.

1. Develop a vision
        Analyse the environment
        Communicate with others regarding the development of a vision
        Inspire others to contribute to the development of a vision
        Secure commitment to the vision
2. Plan to achieve the vision
        Identify strategies
        Plan to implement strategies
        Communicate plan
3. Lead and manage change and continuous improvement
        Implement strategic plan
        Adopt reflective practice
        Adjust strategy as necessary

This set of standards is entitled 'develop strategic practice': this term seems to acknowledge that middle managers develop practice to implement strategy rather than devising strategy themselves. However, the sub-set of activities imply active strategy-making at departmental level.

The insight from this research suggests that middle managers do not devise strategy independently at 'middle' level, and that it could impede their role as corporate agents if they did. It would therefore be helpful to consider the standards within the whole-college setting. We might therefore ask the following questions, based upon the standards and the model.

- How are middle managers enabled to understand the whole-college vision? What forums could you be involved in, which would shape your understanding of the purpose of the college and of whole-college issues, and give you the opportunity to offer your views?
- Do you contribute to whole-college strategy, or is the

strategy 'given' for you to carry out? Are there simple ways in which you could improve the balance?

- How do you then develop a vision at a departmental level, and plan strategically to achieve it? Who do you involve? What factors within the college and external to it do you take into account? How do you motivate others to contribute to the development of the strategy and to carrying it through?

- How do you evaluate the collective contribution of your department to whole-college strategy? How do you adjust the work which you have planned within a changing external and internal environment?

These are big questions. Simply asking them of yourself and of close colleagues – without expecting to find easy answers – can open up valuable layers of thinking. Make an opportunity to discuss one of the question sets above with fellow middle managers or with team members. Air the issues, and identify simple things which can be done. Heightening your awareness of the issues raised throughout this chapter – opening up your corporate role for self-evaluation – will give you a whole-college focus upon the other aspects of your work which are considered in this book.

4 Making it happen

The previous chapter explored the work of middle managers in understanding and carrying out the whole work of the college. This chapter looks more closely at the local aspect of 'making it happen', where the manager acts as an *implementer* of college policy. In terms of the occupational standards for further education leadership and management (Lifelong Learning UK 2005), this aspect of the role includes the responsibility to 'manage and sustain learning and the learning environment' and 'manage resources'.

'The manager's right to manage' cited by, among others, Gleeson and Shain (1999), is seen in this chapter in its working context. Middle managers have an obligation to manage, over a wide range of responsibilities, and to a large extent this is uncontested by the managers and their teams in this study. Carrying out implementation involves sustaining a sense of purpose and direction for the department. As one senior manager at College B puts it, middle managers create 'a vision and an identity for their area of work', an area of activity which was considered at the end of the previous chapter.

For many middle managers, implementation is the most visible aspect of their role. If it is not performed – within the required time-frame – the resulting lack of action is noticeable: something does not happen. This leads to pressure, or role strain: a feeling that there is simply too much to do, and that they are noticeably performing inadequately. The largely 'managerial' nature of the activities can also be discouraging. Some managers express enthusiasm for setting up and operating systems, but for many it is either a chore or logistically difficult. However, middle managers responding to this research enjoyed working creatively and flexibly within apparently mechanical systems. They demonstrated a satisfaction with successful outcomes which sustained their self-image as professional educators.

Making things work: systems and structures

When team members in this research were asked what their manager's role was, the most commonly used phrase was the 'smooth running' of the department. They listed a multitude of routine operational tasks: managing learning resources, finance, space and staff (Student service team member, College A), booking rooms, planning programmes, attending meetings and balancing budgets (Curriculum team member, College B).

Implementation is essentially about 'making things work': this can be perceived as a departmental responsibility, as the first quotation below shows, a function of the college quality systems, as in the second, or as part of all managers' commitment to enacting the purpose of the college, as in the third.

> I ensure that the tasks that our teams need to complete happen at the times they are meant to happen and in the way they are meant to happen. (Service manager, College B)

> Ensure all standards of quality are met, and any changes of procedures are passed on promptly. (Curriculum team member College D)

> Enabling students to learn and to achieve and have a good experience: I think that our managers are really committed to that. (Senior manager, College B)

Implementation, like corporate agency, depends upon the manager's ability to work within the college networks and structures, and to create and manage its operational systems. It depends upon the quality of the systems themselves, and the clarity of the role which managers are trying to implement. Systems which are hard to comprehend or are inconsistent across the college cause frustration, as they erode managers' time and energy. While they reject excessive bureaucracy, the managers in the case-study colleges welcome systems which are standard and coherent.

The things that have to be standard across [the college] are
We know that we need to conform to the requirements ...
at the time stated, so that shapes what you are doing.
(Curriculum manager College A)

Implementing college systems reveals aspects of practice
which need to be improved or developed. One of the criticisms
of managerialism is that it makes people conform to systems,
and reduces professional control (Randle and Brady 1997).
However, systems are created by people, and it is part of the
role of managers and their teams to evaluate the quality of the
college systems, and work to improve them. Systems which
enable implementation to be carried out efficiently can result in
increased professionalism.

Effective implementation involves effective communication,
and this is difficult to operate across a large college where
communication lines are stretched, or when the college is
strongly 'compartmentalized' into areas of provision. Electronic
communication has brought benefits, but staff do not always
access and read the necessary information on the college
intranet or their email, and managers complain that communication does not reach them. Communication gaps occur,
often caused by an overload of information and by the lack of
time, perceived necessity and motivation to access it.

 Reality check

- Which college systems annoy you most? What can you do
  to change them? How could you make the systems work
  better, for you and for others?
- What college systems are you responsible for? How do
  you make them clear for others to follow? How do you
  incorporate feedback to improve them?
- Most colleges have problems with communication. Think
  of one thing which could be done to improve communication – and collaborate with others to do it.

Bureaucracy

There is a fine balance between systems which, through their clarity and predictability make the manager role quicker and easier to implement, and those which, through their impenetrability and lengthiness produce slowness of response and frustration for the manager. The latter type is inevitably labelled as bureaucracy. Managers are scornful about systems which take up time, when time is what they lack:

> If I'm asked to complete Form SBS/2, I would say that prevents me from doing [my job]. (Student service manager, College D)

Bureaucracy cannot only seem lengthy, it can also seem pointless, a barrier to professionalism, as indicated by the comments below. The first manager was not simply questioning the absurdity of the college's quality procedures, he was questioning the validity of the evaluation tool used by the college.

> I think you can do too much navel contemplation in finding out how satisfied people are, whether they are 'very', 'mildly', or just 'moderately' satisfied, and I would question the validity of such data. (Service manager College D)

The next manager pointed out how sometimes a centralized, standardized system can be inappropriate; systems sometimes need to be organically adaptable to local circumstances.

> I think it is unnecessarily burdened by paperwork, and I don't think our Senior Management Team assist things by insisting on a set format, because very often a set format is not applicable for all areas. (Curriculum manager, College D)

Within an organization of the size and complexity of FE colleges, it is difficult to conceive of a bureaucracy which would suit all needs. The case-study colleges in which managers appeared to be most frustrated by bureaucracy were the largest (College C) and the smallest (College D): level of bureaucracy in this case does not seem to correlate with size. The main messages apparent from the research are that managers must be

able to understand and relate to the rationale for a given procedure, must have the time and clarity of instruction to carry it
out, and must feel that the procedure exists to help them as
managers to implement something efficiently.

Reality check

FE is the most bureaucratized of the educational sectors (Centre
for Excellence in Leadership 2005). Much of this bureaucracy
springs from its systems of audit and reporting to external
bodies. Make a list of the reports which you have to make in
order to satisfy this external accountability. How could you
streamline the work on this list, or collaborate with others to
enable tasks to be done more easily?

If you also complete internal reports or supply data which do
not seem to relate to external accountability, what is their
purpose? Do they help you and your colleagues to work more
effectively? Talk to a senior colleague about the list of all the
tasks you have to do.

Resources

'Making it happen' requires resources. There were very few
positive remarks made about levels of resource in FE, either
from middle or senior managers, in this research. Senior
managers tended to talk about enabling managers to manage
resources better, or about the need to communicate reasons for
a lack of resources more clearly. In their research on FE, Hewitt
and Crawford (1997) report the views of senior managers who
were very concerned with the survival of their college, con-
trasting these with the perspectives of lecturers who seemed to
have no understanding of the financial framework within
which senior managers operated. There were elements of this
situation at the case-study colleges. Largely the middle managers understood that there are externally imposed resource
constraints: 'We're cut to the bone everywhere' (Service
manager, College A). However, they often lacked essential
knowledge about how resources were allocated internally, and
some managers had no clear knowledge of their own budget.

'Poor resourcing', for middle managers, is inevitably equated with poor staffing levels, including a lack of access to administrative and technician support. Managers may wish for money to be spent upon improved teaching and office environments, but mainly they wish for it to be spent upon increasing staffing. At College B, in particular, the effect of recent redundancies meant that departments, coping with a growing student population, were under-resourced compared with earlier times. At College C, there was an issue about the non-replacement of staff who had left.

Managers and their teams felt the impact of systemic resource deprivation: resources were not being withheld, they simply did not exist to a great enough degree within the system. Middle managers who had not been part of the internal resource allocation process saw themselves as the 'victims' of change, rather than as making informed decisions about how to manage the reduced resource.

The lack of resource within the sector, and the national focus on efficiency rather than effectiveness (Simkins 2000), can only be resolved at government level. At a college level, the situation can be mediated by good communication about how resource decisions are made, and by discussion to secure the best possible 'fit' between the resource available in the system and the multiple needs which have to be met.

 Reality check

Do you hold your own budget, or do you, as some of the case-study managers do, depend upon a 'Father Christmas' approach to budgeting, not knowing how much is in the sack, or whether it will be available when you need it?

Do you liaise with the college finance office to help you to understand and manage your budget?

Is there an allocation for staffing within your budget, or is staffing determined centrally? Do you know how to bid for new or replacement staff?

Overload

The shortage of resources, and therefore of staff, impacts directly upon the middle managers themselves, potentially causing role ambiguity and overload. It involves them in combining their management role with an operational role, such as teaching, supporting students or handling data. Delegation of duties to overworked staff becomes logistically and ethically difficult, and can conflict with the managers' professional values and judgement:

> I don't think the number of staff that we have reflects the amount of students that we have in the college ... If we have more staff to work, of course our service to the students could be much more effective. (Student service manager, College A)

The most visible effect of a lack of resource is role overload: having too many different things to implement within the time and resources available. This can lead to a minimalist approach, in which managers aim to get as much work as possible done to a basic standard:

> I think that the workload is such that it is very, very hard to do more than deliver. (Senior manager, College B)

The situation puts particular pressure on middle managers, who feel that they will be judged negatively if they do not succeed in delivering to everyone's expectations. Managers may be impeded in their work by the seeming urgency of other people's needs, by trying to operate responsively in unrealistic circumstances. Their resulting anxiety is symptomatic of role overload in which, as Khan *et al.* (1964, p. 25) comment, the manager 'may be taxed beyond the limit of his abilities':

> Its sheer volume sometimes means that to be effective can be very difficult. I really feel quite strongly that the sheer volume of work is overpowering. (Curriculum manager, College D)

> The phone just needs to ring, or you get an email and [your work plan] all goes out of the window ... you're transferring

those things onto your list. (Student service manager, College A)

They can't teach properly because every ten minutes they are being called out of the classroom to manage a crisis. (Senior manager, College C)

In the last two quotations above, the demands upon the middle managers were out of control, resulting in 'sent role' conflict. The managers could not respond flexibly and contingently to the mass of demands which they faced, and their responses echo Mintzberg's comments (1990) about the fragmented activities, the constant interruption and pressure for immediate solutions to problems which make up management. Sometimes, humour was the only relief:

On a good week you would have an overview of all that is going on and try and anticipate part of it – on a good week [laughter]. (Curriculum manager, College D)

One senior manager related this type of pressure to the managers' relative nearness to students. He commented that managers performing curriculum or student service roles have less control of their workload, and more demands on their flexibility, than those whose roles have less direct interaction with students:

They have different problems ... It's the ones that touch students and the ones who don't. Because the ones that don't have larger amounts of control over their jobs as opposed to the ones that touch students. (Senior manager, College B)

This constant need for responsiveness and flexibility links with comments from a senior manager at College C, in relation to the people-centred role of colleges:

I honestly believe that colleges really more than any other part of the education system are about that kind of huge mass of diverse messy humanity. (Senior manager, College C)

For this senior manager, a transformational approach to leadership, which allows for a flexible, organic response to the 'messiness' of human interaction, was the answer.

Reality check

Managing overload entails managing the expectations of your role set, including yourself. What things could you clarify – with your senior manager, your team and yourself – that would make their expectations more manageable?

Specialist knowledge and expertise

'Making it happen' as a manager involves specialist knowledge and experience. Middle managers who are seen as local experts, or leading professionals, incur respect, which in turn enables them to carry out their role. Managers draw upon the specialisms of their team in order to 'pool' expertise, as they cannot be expert across the range of roles and functions they manage. However, they need access both to subject knowledge and management skills, and in the latter area the manager may have less expertise to draw upon. Senior managers at all the colleges speak about the 'mixed ability' of their managers, and of management posts sometimes being a 'reward' for good service, rather than being offered on the basis of management skills or professional potential.

Specialist expertise is needed, not just for implementing on a day-to-day basis; there is the need to be proactive, to take the lead on new ventures, and develop the service or teaching area. Managers have to enhance their specialist knowledge, in such areas as funding changes and new legislation. 'We also have a duty ... to be moving the service forward ... because we are the specialists, senior management aren't' (Student service manager, College A). In contrast, some managers showed an inability to adopt this proactive stance:

> It's a constant frustration ... that one can't spend enough time being proactive and planning and putting strategies into place, because one is spending too much time reacting. Firefighting. (Student service manager, College B)

What is needed to enhance managers' specialist expertise and enable them to view their management role as a profession? Lumby (1997) notes that FE managers accept that the amateur approach to management is no longer applicable. Reluctant managers – and there were some in this survey – may feel that their profession is to be a teacher or to provide a service to students, and in their eyes being a manager is a different type of profession, to which they may not aspire. This issue is discussed further in Chapter 9.

 Reality check

- What do you feel is your specialist area of expertise? Is it an area of knowledge, is it particular skills in management, or a combination of both?
- What is your profession? How would you describe it to others? What is it based upon?
- How does your position as a manager draw upon your areas of expertise and your professionalism? How could you carry out your manager role more professionally?

Summary

To implement effectively, middle managers need to be well placed within the systems and structures of the college. This 'placing' can include ready access to electronic communication and data systems. Middle managers also need an ability to understand and relate to the rationale of the college's bureaucratic systems, including the rationale for resource allocation. Conversely, managers also need the opportunity to shape and define their own role, to be allowed space for creativity in implementation, and to access and use others' specialist knowledge in addition to their own.

Implementation depends upon managers working within a context which enables them to reconcile managerial and professional demands. Their definition of professionalism is likely to vary between the three roles considered here. Curriculum managers are likely to see their professionalism as being rooted in their subject area, rather than in their management skills, whereas increasingly for service and student service managers, there is a perception of professionalism as being rooted both in their service and in how it is managed.

Implementation is impeded by cumbersome college systems which may struggle to operate over multiple college sites and types of college provision. This may be linked to excessive bureaucracy, which erodes both the efficiency and the effectiveness of the college manager. Lack of resources, and a lack of understanding of how resources are allocated, impedes implementation by managers, and constraints on staffing may result in role overload for the manager and team. Managers who are responsible for areas with a high level of student interaction, such as curriculum managers and student service managers, may be subject to stress produced by intensive student need. Managers experience both people-centred pressure and system-centred pressure in their attempts to deal with their workload. Their efforts may be hampered by a lack of management expertise and lack of time to manage, which may increase any pre-existing resistance to carrying out the activities of management.

Modelling implementation

The issues affecting implementation which were identified by college middle managers and their role sets are represented in Figure 5: Modelling implementation.

Key factors which influence the success of managers as implementers include accessibility of data, communication, resources and people. Manager understanding – of the college structures and systems, college bureaucracy and the role itself – is also essential to implementation. A third set of facilitators depends upon professional expertise: the managers' autonomy and skill in shaping their role, and their ability to use the expertise of the whole team to meet the needs of their clients and learners.

As with corporate agency, 'reading' the model can give insight into this aspect of manager activity. Reading down the facilitator side of this model suggests the following proposition:

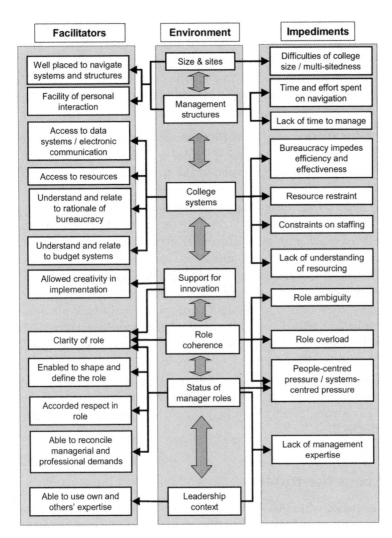

Figure 5 Modelling implementation

if managers are well placed to navigate college systems and structures, they will be enabled in making the personal interaction necessary for the role. Access to data systems, electronic communication and feedback on their role, together with an understanding of college bureaucracy and budget systems will give them the necessary knowledge to carry out the role. The personal interaction and the necessary knowledge, together with clarity given to the role by the college, are used to create and shape the role. Success then depends upon the managers' ability to reconcile the demands placed upon them and to use their own and others' expertise, supported by the respect of others, to carry out the role effectively.

This reading can be used to work through an example at College B, where the strong faculty system made it difficult to navigate cross-college systems and structures. The effect was principally felt by service and student service managers, but also by the curriculum managers themselves, 'isolated' within their faculties. The college was also moving from a transformational style of leadership, established over many years, towards a more transactional one. The managers' clarity of roles and the amount of freedom they had to shape their roles were affected by the change of style and the instability of the college. It is likely, therefore, that middle managers were not well placed to implement effectively, as they lacked clarity and certainty about their roles, and their access to each other was impeded. Once the college has stabilized to its new style of leadership, the clarity and certainty should improve. It would be useful at that point for the college to examine the benefits and disadvantages of its strong faculty system, in order to optimize managers' effectiveness.

Using the model

Try using the model to address role overload, which is a common problem for middle managers. The factors most closely linked with overload are those to do with the coherence and status of the role: does the role 'make sense' to the manager, and do they have the authority, respect and trust of others in carrying it out? Overload is linked to pressure from both people and systems, so it is also useful to look at the cluster of facilitators attached to college systems: do managers relate well enough to college bureaucracy and finance systems, and do they have access to appropriate resources? Above all, do they have the knowledge and 'permission' to shape and define their role and be creative in how it is carried out? Are they victims of the systems and of people's expectations, or do they create and adapt systems which they can manage, and manage others' expectations?

Now take this train of thought further by looking at the factor 'able to reconcile professional and managerial demands'. In the model, this element is linked to the cluster of items we have just considered concerning the clarity of the role, its position within the college, and also its status, the respect which others pay to the role, the pressures upon it, and the manager's ability to shape and define it at a local level. All of these elements support the manager's professional and managerial understanding of implementation. This understanding can enable the manager to deal with the impediments presented in this part of the model: role ambiguity and overload, people-centred pressure and systems-centred pressure. Looking outward from this cluster of items, it can be seen that once the status of the role – not simply the political status within the college, but the status within the manager's own mind – is established, managers are better placed to reconcile the managerial and professional demands placed upon them. They are then able to benefit from other facilitators: they may be better able to understand and use the college systems and management structures in order to enact their role, and they may gain insight into how to use their expertise and creativity in effective implementation.

Managers using this model in order to reflect on their role may be able to identify the key element which, for them, would unlock their potential as implementers, and to see how other factors relate to it. For some of the managers interviewed, particularly the service managers, the key element was to be accorded respect in their role; for others, mainly curriculum managers working below head of faculty level, it was to have access to a budget and to understanding of the college financial systems. Having used the model to identify cause and effect of impediments to your role, you can then consider the related sections of the model, to interpret which factors need to be addressed. Use the 'reality check' questions from this chapter to question more deeply key areas of your activity as manager.

This is the most complex of the five models: implementing the work of the college is a complex activity. Take some time to see how the model works for you, and use it to explore the complexity of your own situation. Above all, identify which of the facilitators you have, and which you lack. Can you find ways to gain that missing factor, or to compensate for its omission? Strength in the left-hand column, together with understanding the factors in the central 'environment' column as they exist at your college, can help you to overcome the negative factors on the right.

Linking to the occupational standards

The managers' role as implementer is closely linked to Key Areas B and D of the occupational standards for middle managers: 'Manage and sustain learning and the learning environment' and 'Manage resources' (Lifelong Learning UK 2005) The standards for Key Area B 'Manage and sustain learning and the learning environment' contain the following sub-sets of activities:

1. Develop and sustain services for learners
    Prepare an operational plan
    Implement an operational plan
    Monitor and review progress against a plan
2. Manage quality in the delivery of services
    Manage services
    Review and evaluate services provided
    Develop and sustain a safe, clean and healthy environment
3. Manage human resources to support the provision of services

This sub-set of activities will be considered in the next chapter.

The standards for Key Area D 'Manage finance and resources' list the following sub-sets of activities.

1. Plan resource requirements
   Analyse resources to meet plans
   Secure approval for expenditure and/or income forecasts, budgets, returns and reports
   Evaluate and agree proposals for income and expenditure
   Continuously improve management of information
2. Manage finance
   Monitor and control activities to meet target income
   Control expenditure against budgets

These two sets of standards are interdependent, as the manager cannot effectively develop and sustain services for learners without planning the resource requirements, including the human resource requirements, which will be discussed in the next chapter.

The activities listed in Key Area B, when set against the reality of implementation as seen through the research, seem devastatingly simplistic. To be fair, the standards list whole sets of knowledge and skills which managers need in order to plan and implement services for learners, but the research has revealed a host of college-based issues which can get in the way of smooth implementation, however skilful and knowledgeable the manager may be. The situation in Key Area D is, if anything, even more problematic. Many of the managers interviewed had little understanding of their own budget area or of how college finance was earned and allocated.

Comparing the standards with the model suggests that if the standards are to be met, middle managers first need effective access: to college operational systems, to resources and understanding of college finance, and to essential data and communication systems. They also need to understand clearly what their role is, and be able to manage the expectations of others. They may then be able to carry out the rational planning activities described in the standards.

Assessing yourself against the standards in Key Areas B and D may therefore appear to identify huge areas of personal deficiency which could, according to the model, be impediments caused by the college environment. The impediments have to be addressed before you can become skilled and knowledgeable in ways indicated by the standards. This is a problem which needs to be addressed. One way forward would be to consider the following questions, based on the standards and the model.

- What information do I need in order to plan effectively for my area of college responsibility? What communication routes do I need to obtain that information consistently and helpfully? Which people can help me to identify and obtain information?
- Which college systems are most important to effective implementation of my role? What data do I need in order to evaluate the work of my area? How do I get access to those data and use them effectively? What college systems and people are there to help me?
- How well do I understand the financial basis of the work of my college area? Where is the information held which would enable that understanding? How can I get regular, supportive access to it?

The key to much of this questioning lies with the managers who are senior to you, and managers who operate the data and information systems. It would be useful to seek discussion with them, either as an individual, or as one of a group of managers with similar needs. There is no use in blaming 'them', whoever 'they' may be, or complaining about systems which do not work. You have to be proactive in seeking and shaping change if you are to implement the work of your area of college effectively.

5 Managing people

Implementation, the work of 'making it happen', cannot be carried out by middle managers alone. An important aspect of their role is therefore managing teams of staff to carry out the day-to-day work of the college, or, as the occupational standards state: 'Lead teams and individuals' (Lifelong Learning UK 2005). This chapter considers the role of the middle manager as *staff manager*: a facet of their work which previous research has identified as one of the most difficult things that managers have to do.

For many middle managers, managing staff is carried out intuitively, and therein lies its difficulty. Given the many other demands of their role, and the pressure of work among those whom they manage, following a pattern of instinctive social response may not be enough. Having a supportive team is essential to the manager's effectiveness and, for some, to their personal well-being. The motivation of a team is sustained by good personal relationships with their manager. However, in managing people, middle managers not only have to draw upon a full range of interpersonal skills, they have to keep this aspect of their role in balance with the other demands on their time and expertise. This may require managers to become more detached from those whom they manage and rely upon, and judging and maintaining the appropriate distance may not be easy.

Skills for managing people

Team members in this research emphasized the importance of being managed well, and identified ten people-centred activities undertaken by their manager.

Sharing information with staff
Directing, guiding, coordinating the team
Listening to and understanding staff: knowing their staff
Delegating to staff
Maintaining good teamworking /effective working
  relationships
Monitoring the work of the team
Dealing with inadequate staff
Valuing staff
Having the respect of staff
Supporting staff

These activities ranged from giving information and instruction, through actions which emphasize collegiality, support and mutual respect, through to an acknowledgement that middle managers must delegate to staff, monitor their work and, if necessary, discipline them. According to the team members, these activities demanded a range of interpersonal skills, together with 'personality, commitment and experience' (Curriculum team member, College B). Team members also recognized the importance for the manager of receiving support from the team.

Middle managers spoke at length about this aspect of their role as one which they felt was important, but found difficult. Some of the managers in the study felt that they had a natural affinity with managing people, 'the human side of things' (Student service manager, College D), which was seen as an antidote to servicing college bureaucracy. Those who were more doubtful of their capabilities nevertheless felt an obligation to act responsively towards staff problems, even when 'part of me says, "I wish that person would disappear and take their problem somewhere else"' (Curriculum manager, College B).

The role draws upon a range of skills, 'mentoring, counselling, negotiating, facilitating' (Curriculum manager, College B), learned over many years. Managers tended to use different styles, adapting to the needs of individuals and groups, being directive or transformative in response to context and need:

There are those who need the functional, directional, those who are far happier with the transformational and the creative as well. (Service manager, College C)

The potential effectiveness of this approach is emphasized by Glover *et al.* (1999, pp. 332–3) who identify successful middle managers in schools as those who use 'best fit' approaches, and 'make use of contingency theory when working with individuals'.

The managers' communication skills, together with good college channels of communication, are essential in their role of managing staff. Team members from all the colleges valued managers who maintained good communication with staff in every direction, with students and external bodies, in order to keep their team well informed. This included having regular, efficiently run team meetings in which information was shared. Through being properly informed, team members understood the context of their work better. Senior staff also spoke of the importance of establishing shared understanding in 'trying to let staff know why it is, where we need to go' (Senior manager, College D). Open communication can alleviate the difficulty of middle managers becoming 'piggy in the middle', mediating between the demands of senior management and their team, although many managers saw translating or brokering communication from 'above' and 'below' as an inevitable function of middle management. This issue is dealt with in more detail in Chapter 6.

Reality check

The insight offered by Adair (1983) is useful here. He depicted the work of staff management as interlocking circles: managing the team and the task and the individual.

How do you balance the need to support individual team members with maintaining good working relationships within the team, and keeping a purposeful focus on the task to be done? How do you prevent any one of the 'circles' from taking all of your energy? What would happen if you neglected one of

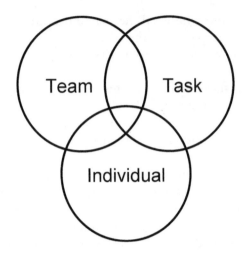

Figure 6 Managing the team, the task and the individual (after Adair 1983)

the circles for too long? What management skills do you feel you are using to keep the whole activity in balance?

Working with people: delegation and protection

Many of the middle managers in this research valued their staff management role. They enjoyed 'working with people', and spoke warmly of the support which they received from their team. For some, the main motivation for their work was derived from this aspect of their role; some said that they would have given up their job if it were not for the willingness of their team. However, they also spoke of the increasing difficulty of working in FE, and of the dependence upon staff to work beyond what might be seen as their contract. Staff with specialist expertise could seek alternative employment: 'I know my employees could be paid a lot more elsewhere and it's not easy' (Service manager, College B). The manager's skill in maintaining goodwill, and the staff's willingness to offer it, are therefore important factors in managing people.

Middle managers depend upon specialist expertise from their team in areas which are beyond their own range, adopting what one service manager describes as a 'democratic' style, in which team members take responsibility for work within their specialism. This is clearly necessary when a curriculum manager is responsible for a wide range of subjects, but it also applies to service and student service managers. One marketing manager noted the different specialisms within her team, including schools liaison, journalism and graphic design (Service manager, College B), and a student service manager spoke of managing: 'welfare officers, careers advisors, youth workers ... they update me on issues that need to be addressed' (Student service manager, College A). Skill from the manager is needed to channel staff energy and commitment into teamwork:

> They are very lively, they're not easy people to manage, they are not 'yes' people by any means, but very mutually supportive and, I should add, supportive of me. (Student service manager, College D)

Managers spoke with warm admiration of their teams: 'When we do something, boy, they are good' (Student service manager, College A), and team members showed willingness to work with managers who attempted to understand staff, who supported the people in their teams, valued them and won their respect.

One curriculum manager commented: 'I think there are a lot of skills to learn and one of them is being able to delegate' (Curriculum manager, College B). Delegation not only spreads the load and potentially disperses leadership further into the organization; it also develops team members' awareness of the working context of the department. Delegation contrasts with the protective approach of the manager who aims to 'buffer' the team from 'paperwork from above', (Curriculum manager, College D), or who tries to prevent overload on a depleted team:

> We've got less people now than we had three years ago, yet we've got more students. And we're the ones in the middle that have to make the two bits match – or not as the case may be. (Student service manager, College B)

Maintaining a balance of work within the team may involve monitoring both the team members' work and their well-being by regulating the level of pressure upon them. Monitoring work, through customer surveys, classroom observation of teaching and checking the work of service and student service team against service standards, has been common practice in colleges since 1997, when annual self-assessment reports were instituted. Monitoring the 'operational health' of the team is a much more intuitive aspect of staff management:

> I have to maintain a team of people, and that means checking that they are actually OK as well as the fact that they are doing their job. (Student service manager, College C)

It also entails stepping in to do the work of the team when necessary, being the 'servant leader' (Brown and Rutherford 1998).

 ## Reality check

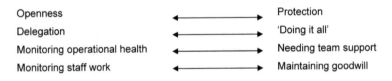

Openness	Protection
Delegation	'Doing it all'
Monitoring operational health	Needing team support
Monitoring staff work	Maintaining goodwill

Figure 7 Managing the team

Different managers operate in different places on the spectra indicated in Figure 7 above. Some of the lines imply a clear choice: 'Do I protect my team from external pressures, or do I tell them everything?' Others indicate that a balance is necessary: 'I need to monitor the work of my staff while maintaining their goodwill.' Personal need can be a deciding factor: 'I actively seek the personal support of the team to carry out my role', as can an ethical stance: 'I cannot delegate to an already over-burdened team.' The stance of the manager depends upon their own personality and upon the college context.

If you are having difficulty in managing staff, consider where you stand on each of these spectra. Which stance is sapping your energy or causing you frustration? What would happen if you moved towards the other end of the line?

Practical problems in managing staff

The systems for employing staff, particularly those on temporary or part-time contracts, were seen by managers and their teams in the case-study colleges as over-bureaucratic, as undervaluing the staff concerned, and as impediments to their role:

> I was told that we didn't get some member of staff because I hadn't filled in the request form by a specific date. Well I never have done [that before], is that my role? Is that what I am supposed to be doing? If it is, fine, I will do it. (Curriculum manager, College C)

Procedures for appointment could involve 'six signatures, I think it is you have to get, one of them being yours' (Curriculum manager College C), and systems for issuing part-time contracts were also seen as unwieldy: 'The whole part-time contract, it creates a huge workload at every level – and it is unworkable' (Curriculum manager, College D).

Curriculum managers are most likely to be managing staff on part-time contracts who may be employed for short periods of the week, at a time or in a place where the manager is not present. They may have difficulties locating, monitoring and supporting people for whom they are responsible, and team meetings may be logistically impossible. Although many part-time staff responding to this research replied that they have good relationships with their manager, a small number indicated that they felt neither known nor valued by their manager, and were ignorant of what their manager does: 'I don't know what she does. She has no understanding of the courses I teach' (Curriculum team member, College B).

Two of the case-study colleges (College A and College C) operate on multiple sites. As a result, some managers spend a lot of time travelling from site to site, with detriment to their health and effectiveness: 'At the end of the day you are knackered and don't feel that you have really achieved anything apart from bouncing around' (Student service manager, College C). Managers at all of the colleges valued face-to-face contact in developing trust and ensuring the mutual understanding needed for effective team management. Their experience supports the view of Howell and Hall-Meranda (1999, p. 683) that 'physical distance decreases the opportunities for direct influence and potentially the effectiveness of the working relationship between leader and follower'.

Curriculum managers are most likely to have their staff on one site, although this is not always the case. Subjects such as adult basic skills or English for speakers of other languages might be taught at a number of main sites and also at community outreach centres. While service managers and their teams may all be based together at one site, their role – for example marketing or estates – entails the manager and team members travelling to other sites to carry out their work. The work of the various services to students – for example, admissions, library services, learning support – may be carried out on every college site. Colleges A and C were both experimenting with site-based or faculty-based staffing for some of these services, in order to minimize travel and to enable more effective management.

 ## Reality check

You cannot solve all of the problems indicated above, but you don't need to be a victim of circumstance either. So choose one problem which you think can be addressed. Talk to your line manager about it, work out a manageable action plan and solve it. Who knows – this may encourage you to try to solve some of the others!

Team relationships: first among equals?

Concern for the team, and support of them, is a key part of the manager's role: one which needs a careful approach to prevent overload for the manager. Giving practical support is important in establishing a positive relationship with team members; managers in this research spoke of obtaining improved access to photocopying or water coolers for their teams, as well as offering time and concern to those who needed it. Social bonding with team members can, however, cause problems for managers, especially when they share a staffroom or have worked with them as colleagues before promotion. One manager realized that she had to deliver the message that 'Just because I am sitting at my desk it doesn't mean you can come to me with "trivia" ' (Curriculum manager, College C).

A senior manager at College A touched on the professionalism needed when managing staff: 'Good management of staff is not about everyone being chummy and going down to the pub. It's about achieving the unit costs or the pass rate or the retention or the curriculum development that you want to achieve' (Senior manager, College A). However much the manager may enjoy 'working with people', the impulse to make friends with the team, and to make allowance for failure and underperformance, may be to the detriment of the college and is not professional practice. This situation may be compounded when managers need to work from within the team, yet also need to distance themselves from team members in order to carry out monitoring and line management activity. This problem was described by a curriculum manager in the following way: 'You are not quite in management with a capital M, you are also with the teaching staff . . . it is a curious sort of path that you tread really' (Curriculum manager, College B).

One senior manager commented on this as the 'first among equals' role: 'They are having to manage and having to be part of the team. You know, the "first among equals" kind of thing, it's just uncomfortable' (Senior manager, College B). A senior manager at College A commented that new middle managers find managing performance and managing conflict as the most difficult parts of their role. Middle managers are often promoted from within their team, and one principal spoke of the rarity of being able to make external appointments at middle-manager level. Managing staff who have recently been colleagues was therefore a feature of middle-manager experience in the case-study colleges. The 'human side of things' may be more difficult than some managers anticipate.

Reality check

Let's face it – you are not 'first among equals', however much you may value the experience and skills of your team members. You are their staff manager. Look at the relationship from that perspective and make whatever adjustments are necessary. The changes will probably be more difficult for you than for the team, but you will all benefit in the long run.

Managing difficult staff

The people-centred aspects of the role, which are valued by many middle managers, can involve a high level of demand upon the manager's time and skills. Managers may experience role strain through an excess of people-centred demands: 'Three teams of people with different problems and expectations and you are trying to deal with them all' (Curriculum manager, College B), or through staff aggression in asserting their needs: 'You felt like you were dropped into an aquarium of piranha fish' (Curriculum manager, College B). Spending too little time considering and meeting staff needs can make the manager feel guilty and unprofessional: 'I don't have enough time to develop individuals, and I am very aware sometimes that development is necessary' (Student service manager, College B). Striking the right balance between supporting staff and carrying out other aspects of the role is a difficult task.

Managing staff who underperform is a particular problem for managers, not least because the systems for dealing with underperformance are lengthy and unwieldy. As one manager in this study pointed out: 'That individual may actually be preventing us from carrying out our overall role as manager effectively ... we all know what a bad member of staff can do to a programme' (Curriculum manager, College B). The member of staff may have been 'inherited' when the manager was appointed, and may have been in post for a considerable number of years. For managers in this study, the process of removing staff was 'a long-term activity' (Curriculum manager, College B), in which initially, according to one manager, 'nobody would do anything' (Curriculum manager, College D). Poor staff performance affects the department's achievement of college targets, and thus impacts upon the effectiveness and perceived professionalism of the manager.

 Reality check

You are not alone in your situation of having to handle difficult staff. Talk to others (in confidence) about the problem: include your personnel manager, line manager and other managers who you know have experience in resolving staffing issues. Take their advice, think clearly what you must do, and use their professional support to bring about a satisfactory outcome. Facing up to the problem – whether it is one of staff underperformance, aggression or unreasonable expectations upon you – can go a long way towards solving it.

Summary

Managing people is facilitated by the managers' interpersonal skills and by their ability to harness the support of the team. It also depends upon access to good college channels of information and data, which can be passed on to the team to clarify their role. It is important that the college structures enable face-to-face contact with the staff being managed. It is also important that the manager is aware of the formal aspects of managing staff, as the team's contribution and conformity to college purposes and systems is taken as a measure of the manager's effectiveness.

Staff management becomes difficult when managers feel the need to protect staff from overload, and worry about the risk of losing them and their specialist expertise. College systems for recruiting, contracting and releasing staff are all seen as unwieldy. Dealing with underperforming staff is also difficult, especially where staff may work on a different site. Inter-site management of staff is a demanding activity; paradoxically, managing from within a close-knit team can also present problems. Above all, the manager is buffeted by the complexity of staff needs, each of which demands a differentiated response. Curriculum managers and some student service managers are also likely to have large teams to manage, which likewise increases the difficulty for them of this aspect of role.

Modelling staff management

Figure 8 depicts the staff manager aspect of role. The interpersonal skills of the manager and the support and professionalism of the team are the engine which drives this aspect of role. What the model also shows are the underpinning formal elements. If the management structures of the college are unhelpful, for example, and the manager role is not clear,

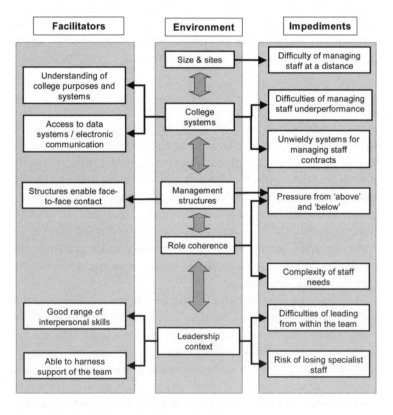

Figure 8 Modelling staff management

the manager can be faced with conflicting demands from the senior management and the team, the classic 'piggy in the middle' situation. As the literature indicates that this is a common problem for any middle manager, colleges might usefully examine the relationship between the managers at different levels and the departmental teams, including their mutual expectations.

Looking at the second cluster in the model, the college systems supporting staff management are mainly apparent when they malfunction and become impediments. Managers, concerned to maintain the balance of relationships represented in the final cluster of the model, become frustrated when formal systems fail to support them, for example over the issuing of contracts. For curriculum managers, who are most likely to manage staff on a number of types of contract, this element becomes burdensome, putting the role 'out of balance'.

A useful way of evaluating the staff manager aspect of role is to read down the facilitator side of the model:

> College structures should be set up which optimize face-to-face interaction between managers and their teams, and systems be designed to provide efficient access to data and electronic communication. If the managers then have a good understanding of the college purposes and systems, and a good range of interpersonal skills, they should be able to harness the support of their team and manage staff to the benefit of the college.

If the staff manager role is largely undertaken intuitively, managers may not see that their team needs to be managed within the framework of college purposes and systems. They would probably see the need for strong interpersonal skills, but it might be harder for them to identify that they are not making the best use of the systems and communication routes available to them.

Using the model

A simple reading of the whole model may improve understanding of the context within which staff management is set, and help to identify areas for manager or whole-college development. These could include a sharing of managers' strategies for leading from within a team or for managing staff at a distance, an examination of the systems for employing staff and for storing and retrieving data concerning them, or a re-examination of the expectations and pressures upon middle managers.

As with the other models, looking at a single cluster can also provide insight. The top cluster can be analysed in relation to College A, which was moving to a more site-based management system. Senior managers hoped to achieve three objectives by this change of structure: decentralization of college management, identification of staff with particular college centres and easier access of managers to their teams. The difficulty of managing staff at a distance would be alleviated for curriculum managers (although to a certain extent they were centre-based before the change), and for some student service managers, such as those managing student admissions, who would be responsible for services only on one site. Other student service managers, such as the learning resources manager, would still have their team scattered among the sites. Service managers would have their teams adjacent to them, but would be providing services, such as finance and human resources, to all sites. The solution is thus seen as a compromise between the benefits gained by most managers of being adjacent to the staff they manage and the costs of dispersing leadership out into the college centres.

Linking to the occupational standards

Staff management is highlighted in one aspect of Key Area B of the occupational standards, and the whole of Key Area C 'Lead teams and individuals' (Lifelong Learning UK 2005). The subset of activities for Key Area B 'Manage and sustain learning and the learning environment' is as follows:

3. Manage human resources to support the provision of services
    Identify and meet requirements for staff
    Ensure efficient and effective deployment of staff resources

The activities set out in Key Area D 'Lead teams and individuals' are as follows.

1. Manage and develop self and own performance
    Manage self
    Develop self
2. Maintain and develop team and individual performance
    Promote the organisation's values and vision to staff and students
    Advise and support teams and individuals
    Assess effectiveness of teams and individuals
    Contribute to staff development and training
3. Build and maintain productive working relationships
    Secure the respect, trust and support of colleagues, students and external contacts
    Deal professionally with conflict between colleagues and /or students
    Contribute to the promotion of the organisation and sector

The activities in Key Area D outlined above also address liaison and leadership responsibilities which will be discussed in the next two chapters.

The activities in Key Area B concern the management of staff as a resource. Some of the issues underpinning this aspect of management were discussed in the previous chapter. If the resource allocated to the college or to the department is insufficient for the service which is to be provided, then overload results, either for the middle manager in trying to address the mismatch or for the whole team in trying to meet the shortfall. In this chapter, issues concerning staff underperformance were discussed: this, too can lead to ineffective and inequitable deployment of staff and consequent overload.

The first set of activities in Key Area D will be discussed in Chapter 7. The second set echoes the Adair model discussed earlier in this chapter of maintaining the task, the team and the individual. The way in which the manager would 'promote the organisation's values and vision to staff and students' would be to make sure that the task – of providing for student learning – was properly understood and undertaken.

The other activities concern the development, support and monitoring both of teams and individuals. It is important to note, however, the tensions between these three activities. When a manager has to spend time and energy addressing the needs of individual members of staff, the needs of the team and the task may be sidelined. Likewise, a task may be so important to the success of the department that it occupies the whole of the manager's focus, leaving the team and the individuals within it unsupported. Ironically, this undermines the successful completion of the task.

Both the standards and the model demonstrate the balance of interpersonal and managerial skills which are needed to manage staff effectively. Team members cannot be developed and supported professionally if the manager has little understanding of the college systems for contracting, appraising and monitoring staff, or of the college purpose which they must carry out.

Self-evaluation questions for middle managers, based on the standards and the model, could therefore be as follows.

- How can I best understand and present the purpose of the college, and therefore of this department, to my team?
- How can I best secure resources for effective staffing and deployment? What choices do I have here? Who can advise me?
- What systems can I adopt which will help me to manage and monitor staff in a humane and equitable way? What do other middle managers do? How can I learn from them?

- How can I best keep the task, the team and the individual in balance? Do I need to alter my approach to any of these three, so that all three are better supported?
- Do I have to manage staff on my own? Who, within the college, and within the team, is there to help me?

This last question highlights the fact that middle managers do not manage in isolation. It therefore leads us to consider in the next chapter the issue of liaison.

6 Working together

The previous chapter looked at the interaction of managers and their teams in implementing the work of the college. In this chapter, we look more widely across the college and beyond it, to consider the *liaison* aspect of the middle-manager role.

If implementation and staff management are at the core of the middle-manager role, liaison is a key means by which it is carried out. Many middle managers work with other teams on a regular basis, either to implement curriculum provision or to integrate college services to support the curriculum:

> You go to somebody and say what do you want? And then you go to other middle managers ... and we interpret that [in terms of accommodation and IT provision] so the dialogue between middle managers again is crucial. (Service manager, College B)

The manager above illustrates that, for the student to have a successful educational experience, the various college functions have to fit together and work as a coherent whole. Because liaison involves managers in interactions with people over whom they do not have direct authority, it brings into play issues of power, status and territoriality. Liaison can therefore be a highly political arena where other people's agendas and assumptions must be understood and dealt with in order to manage effectively.

Vertical liaison: bridging and brokering

For team members, their manager's most visible liaison is vertical, up and down the college hierarchies, acting as a conduit for information and as a mediator with senior management:

'Staff have the certainty of knowing … that their concerns are made known to senior managers' (Student service team member, College A); managers 'mediate between the people who actually do the work and those who institute unworkable policies' (Curriculum team member, College A). Team members rely on their manager to be an advocate and resource finder for the department, 'to fight their corner' (Service team member, College C), to 'argue our corner and achieve stuff for us' (Curriculum team member, College A).

For the manager, vertical liaison presents problems. Middle management classically takes place in 'that layer in the middle where it's coming down and it's going up and there is a crunch point in the middle' (Senior manager, College B). Managers in different roles and different colleges used similar language to describe being caught between multiple sets of pressures from senior managers and their team: 'piggy in the middle', 'buffered from both sides', 'pressurized', 'a buffer', 'an arbiter between those two pressures'. One student service manager took the idea of 'middleness' still further, by identifying student services as being at the crossing point of both the vertical and lateral structures of the college, mediating between senior managers and team members, curriculum and college service functions: 'I suppose perhaps we more than anybody are in the middle' (Student service manager, College D). A student service manager at a different college expressed the intensity of this experience of 'sent role' conflict: 'It is like everybody else in the organization is after you' (Student service manager, College A).

This middle role entails both bridging and brokering. Bridging involves the manager being an active conduit for views and information:

Push those problems upwards so senior managers see them. (Student service manager, College B)

Bridge the gap between senior management and teaching staff'. (Curriculum manager, College A)

This last comment implies a gulf between the senior managers and team members, to be spanned by the activities of the middle manager. An intensification of this 'bridging' aspect of liaison is 'brokering': the 'wheeling and dealing' necessary in order to progress the work of the department. A student service manager at College D spoke about acting as a 'salesman' in his cross-college liaison role, having to 'drag out the benefits of what you want to do, and make sure they understand that the benefit's all theirs'. Another spoke of brokering between senior managers and his team:

> Trying to learn to give senior managers what they are looking for, what they need – or just enough of that – involves all kinds of ... manipulation, subterfuge. (Student service manager, College B)

This quotation illustrates the art of strategic compliance, described by Gleeson and Shain (1999, p. 482), as an 'artful pragmatism, which reconciles professional and managerial interests'.

Reality check

Research into middle management indicates that the situation of being 'piggy in the middle' comes with the role. One way of addressing the situation can be to think through what the benefits might be: to see the situation of being in the middle as an influential and creative one, rather than being a hard-pressed victim.

Think about instances where you have 'bridged the gap' between senior management and your team effectively. What were you trying to achieve? Why did it work? What 'missing element' did you supply? What can you learn from this success?

Lateral liaison: spanning college structures

Vertical liaison is complemented by lateral liaison, which involves spanning gaps between the systems and structures of the college. Liaison is easiest in situations in which managers are located in the same part of the building: in a multi-site college, managers work together most readily within sites: 'They tend to work as a centre cluster' (Senior manager, College A).

Liaison is also enhanced by positive experience of working together:

> If they get good service from another manager ... they are more likely to work better with them the next time. (Senior manager, College D)

Managers at Colleges A and C spoke of this relationship of trust persisting when they moved to other college sites; the previous experience of working together held the key to new patterns of liaison. Working 'against the grain' of college structures, however, is not easy. Some service and student managers in this research had created their own systems for inter-departmental liaison, linking their team members with curriculum teams to promote collaborative management of tasks such as providing learning resources and managing student admissions.

Whereas many managers had relatively clear-cut responsibilities for implementing curriculum or service or student service functions, some had roles which were to a certain extent 'mixed'. For example, curriculum manager roles had been integrated with an element of service or student service management at College C: this helped liaison, particularly between managers at different sites. At Colleges B and D, inter-site working was less of a problem, but there was strong demarcation between faculties, and working with a manager outside one's own area could be culturally or logistically difficult. Managers spoke of having to 'knock on doors and get across' the structure of the college (Student service manager, College D), sometimes without any feeling of authority: 'You may be dealing with your peers ... you haven't necessarily got the authority to influence them' (Service manager, College C). In this situation, liaison is most difficult for those with service and student service functions, as they have to negotiate the co-operation of each faculty separately. They are trying to establish working relationships which are impeded by the structure of the college. The various sections of the college, whether they are faculties or sites or services, inevitably create their own working environments, which can be difficult for others to penetrate. Ease of inter-section working is lost, and with it the means of creating coherent whole-college provision.

Senior managers emphasized the importance of cross-college liaison, of trying to avoid a 'silo mentality' (Senior manager, College C). They spoke of trying to foster liaison through the organization of college management systems, for example on a centre basis (Senior manager, College A) or on a non-hierarchical basis (Senior manager, College C), or by bringing managers with different roles into meetings together and valuing them equally (Senior manager, College C). They also saw it as their own role to 'unblock' problems of liaison (Senior manager, College A). One senior manager observed the importance of cross-college liaison in enabling colleges to be responsive:

> The nimble organization has got these cross-routes of communication ... because you get things done by removing those barriers. (Senior manager, College B)

This senior manager also described how the various patterns of liaison experienced by middle managers help them to understand and shape their role, in effect illustrating the impact of the 'role set' upon the manager:

> When I'm talking about communication, I don't just mean their talking, it is information they get ... the people they communicate to and with on a regular basis ... I think if anything that shapes a person's role. (Senior manager, College B)

 ## Reality check

Some of the managers in the research rarely worked with others across the college, yet all could see that this type of liaison was needed. Think about the factors which help you to work across the college: knowing other managers; understanding their work; being located near them. How can you develop and strengthen this aspect of your work?

Influence of senior managers

Senior managers can be influential in enabling middle managers to work together, especially where there are territorial or power issues. Liaison between senior managers can help to bridge the gap:

> If you have got a good relationship with your manager and your management team, you know your life is made a lot easier ... if the communications are good between [senior managers] as well. (Curriculum manager, College B)

Having a champion at senior manager level can help to make things happen, as the proposed action is seen as being for the good of the college: 'Other staff know that "it's not just you on a power trip"' (Service manager, College D). The position of senior managers gives added support to the activities of the middle manager; a student service manager at College D spoke of the 'game' he played when sending memos to other managers, of putting 'copied to' a senior manager, whether he actually copied the memo or not. Liaison with the supporting power of a senior manager is more effective.

Senior managers at College C helped middle managers to address the 'bouncing ball' syndrome, in which a problem is passed on without managers addressing it properly themselves:

> It's very easy just to bounce the ball between finance, personnel, head of faculty and then back; and while that's happening nothing's moving. (Senior manager, College C)

In similar terms, one senior manager at College A spoke of the progress that has been made from a previous culture in which:

> in the end of the year reviews, people would write down jobs for the Heads of Services ... there's great long lists of jobs for other people to do. (Senior manager, College A)

Both of the senior managers quoted above felt that these negative cultures had been addressed through fostering effective liaison and a stronger culture of accountability.

Sometimes working together was simply seen as common sense:

A head of school would have no problems in picking up a phone to a head of service. (Senior manager, College A)

I encourage this layer to speak to the head of human resources and the head of resources ... there's no point them coming to me and me talking to them and then it's coming round in circles. (Senior manager, College D)

This resonates with the analysis of 'radix organizations' presented by Schneider (2002), in which there is an emphasis upon lateral relationships across functions. While there are aspirations to these kinds of networks and relationships, the middle manager responses to this research indicate that successful operation on this basis is difficult to sustain.

 ## Reality check

Who are your senior management champions? How assertively do you use them? Your senior manager may need to know how best to help you liaise with others; the problems are not always obvious.

How can you and your fellow managers address the 'bouncing ball syndrome'? How can you ensure that you and others 'catch the ball' and address the problem, rather than just moving it on? How might your senior managers help in this?

Status and territory: blame cultures

Curriculum managers, who carry responsibility for the fundamental activities of teaching and learning, are often perceived to hold superior status, unless the college makes proactive efforts to redress the balance. Comments about lack of authority in role and an undervaluing of their professionalism tend to come from service and student service managers; it is managers in these roles who report most difficulty in liaison, and who suffer from 'blame cultures'. Paradoxically, because of their 'local' concern for a particular curriculum area, curriculum managers are often perceived as having less of a 'whole-college' view than their colleagues in service or student service roles, and college approaches to target-setting which set up competition between faculties can lead to competitive demands upon service and student service resource.

In part, this difficulty of liaison between different types of manager is perceived as 'historical', dating back to pre-incorporation, when colleges carried out fewer of their own administrative functions, and the role of administrative staff was seen as less important. The situation is compounded by the growing 'professionalization' of service and student service functions. Colleges are increasingly likely to appoint people with professional experience in these roles, or to encourage role-holders to develop professional expertise.

Moreover, as a senior manager in College A points out, managers holding service and student service responsibilities are actually 'nearer' to the senior management team in their lines of communication and accountability than curriculum heads. The potential for authority in role for service and student service managers has therefore been growing, and has been recognized by senior managers. This results in additional frustration when curriculum managers do not recognize their new and growing status.

Lack of knowledge of others' working environments within the different sections of the college can also lead to blame cultures. Key college services tend to be singled out for criticism, as their perceived malfunction can have an impact right across the college. There is usually a valid reason for the initial concern; the situation then escalates until the manager or department is blamed automatically, whatever the circumstances. For example, at two of the case-study colleges, managers reported that concerns about their college Management Information Services had generated a blame culture. This situation had led to a review of the service and modification of the data systems to make them more accessible for managers. The valid reason for blame had been removed, and managers largely commended the new service.

Reality check

Issues of status and territory get in the way of managers valuing each other's roles and working together effectively. If there are blame cultures at your college, they may need to be addressed on a whole-college basis, by means of developments led by your senior managers. At a local level, you can break down barriers through working together for mutual respect. Try to bring problems out into the open, and point out specific whole-college benefits of working more collaboratively and equitably.

Summary

Although liaison is difficult to achieve, most respondents saw it as essential to the coherent function of the college, the presentation of the 'whole jigsaw' of provision to the individual student. Working together can be enabled through well-planned location of staff: by managers being located near to their own team and to other key managers. Where proximity is not possible, liaison can also be enabled by the managers' location within cross-college working teams. Working together is strengthened through managers' mutual respect, and through them valuing each other's roles within the whole purpose of the college. Senior managers are key agents in promoting inter-manager liaison.

Although liaison might be regarded as a largely mechanical activity, in which the manager uses college structures and systems to undertake collaborative activity, many of the impediments to liaison stem from the managers' attitudes, value systems and scope for understanding others in the system. The difference in difficulty experienced by different types of manager is most evident in this aspect of role. Student service and service managers are most likely to be involved in cross-college liaison, yet the structures and power bases of the college, based upon curriculum areas or sites, do not usually favour managers in these roles. Their roles are sometimes seen as having lesser status than those of curriculum managers, and this impedes equitable liaison.

Modelling liaison

Liaison between managers is underpinned by the college's collective ability to work as a coherent whole. Managers are supported in working together by easy access to, and co-operation from, teams and managers across the college structure. Taken as a whole, the model displayed in Figure 9 seems to indicate that, in practice, liaison is mainly facilitated by systems and impeded by people. In other words, the enabling factors which may exist in the whole-college systems can be impeded by the locally focused systems and purposes devised by other managers. This factor operates right across the model: for example, the manager gains little benefit from being located close to those with whom liaison is needed, if the potential partners do not trust and value the manager or their role.

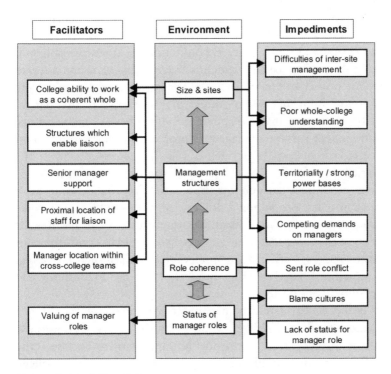

Figure 9 Modelling liaison

This situation is clarified when we read the impediments presented in the model:

> Difficulty of management across the site, or between sites, compounded by attitudes of territoriality and competing demands on manager services, makes a poor basis for effective liaison. The situation may be exacerbated by poor whole-college understanding, which can lead to blame cultures and a lack of status and respect being accorded to the full range of middle managers. Liaison is thus effectively impeded.

Using the model

A useful example can be worked through in relation to College D. At this college, the curriculum managers, placed within powerful faculties, were accorded respect and status within their role. However, the extent of their power impeded managers of other types, who had little status in the eyes of curriculum managers, and who received conflicting, competitive demands from them. Service and student service managers were deterred by the power and territoriality of the curriculum managers, and therefore their success was impeded. There was a further danger in this situation, that the apparent ineffectiveness of the service and student service managers reinforced the curriculum managers' lack of respect for them. This led to an erosion of the clarity of role for the service and student service managers, as curriculum managers attempted to 'take over' some parts of their roles, producing a downward spiral of effectiveness for the college as a whole. From this discussion, it can be inferred that what is needed for success are optimal conditions for all managers, rather than preferential conditions for some, and senior managers may hold the key to establishing this collaborative culture.

If the faculty-based management structures are valued as a framework for the college – and given the educational purpose of the college, this is a reasonable framework to choose – the college needs to address the deficiency in whole-college understanding and the differential value placed upon manager roles which are preventing effective liaison. In the words of the first item in the model: the college needs to address how it is to work as a coherent whole.

The model shows that the systemic support needed for liaison is relatively simple. Both the management structures and the college operating systems need to offer opportunities for managers to work together: laterally across the manager roles and vertically between senior managers and teams. As was seen earlier at College A, choices have to be made over proximal location which will inevitably enable some liaison routes and block others. This situation can be mediated, as in College C, by managers working together on projects in cross-college, cross-functional teams. The top and bottom items in the facilitator column are crucial: there has to be a unity of college design and a mutual valuing of roles if the different aspects of college function which the various managers represent are to be enabled to work together as a coherent whole.

Linking to the occupational standards

The liaison aspect of the middle-manager role is mainly addressed in a sub-set of activities set out in Key Area C 'Lead teams and individuals' (Lifelong Learning UK 2005).

 2. Build and maintain productive working relationships
Secure the respect, trust and support of colleagues, students and external contacts
Deal professionally with conflict between colleagues and/or students
Contribute to the promotion of the organization and sector

It must also be acknowledged that many of the activities in the occupational standards entail effective liaison. For example, the sub-set of activities in Key Area B: 'Manage quality in the delivery of services' cannot be undertaken without liaison, although this aspect of the middle-manager role is generally under-emphasized in the standards.

The main focus of this chapter and of the model has been on the statement in Key area C: 'Build and maintain productive working relationships'. The standards require middle managers to have effective consultation strategies and to build and maintain networks. The material in this chapter has helped us to consider how these networks can be established and maintained, and what prevents them from forming and working effectively. Using the model, we can see that where the manager is placed and how the manager's role is valued are key issues for effective liaison. Possible approaches to improving liaison between managers are as follows.

- In Chapter 2, you were invited to think about the college structures, and where you are placed within them. Use that thinking to draw your own web of liaison within the college. Put yourself at the centre, and draw lines to the teams and individuals that you need to liaise with. Draw thick lines where liaison is good, thin ones where it is satisfactory, and dotted lines where it needs to be strengthened.
- Firstly, look at the thick lines. Why is this liaison easy? Do you simply get on well with these people? Is your office base near them? Is your work very dependent upon theirs? Do they value you and your work?
- What is different about the dotted lines? Is the liaison simply less important and less regular, or do you need to build these links more strongly? What can you learn from the links with the thick lines?

You may need to be more proactive in building the weaker links, and may need to break down some of the barriers discussed in this chapter. What is encouraging in this research is that, in situations in which managers have made the effort to work together for a particular purpose, the links remain strong even when the need for liaison is less. Personal respect has been established, and the cooperative relationship can be restored very easily when it is needed.

7 Middle managers as leaders

Are FE middle managers *leaders*? This issue is problematic. Until recently, the term 'leader' has been little used in FE colleges, apart from the first line manager role of 'team leader'. Leadership as a concept has not been significantly on the agenda. As Lumby (2001, p. 13) comments:

> The current climate where the role of manager is often not viewed positively and leadership is rarely discussed, makes the interpretation of the role of leader/manager in the sector more difficult.

However, with the advent of the Centre for Excellence in Leadership as the leadership college for the sector, and the reissuing of the occupational standards as standards for both leadership and management, leadership as a concept may be more readily accepted. The size and complexity of FE colleges certainly require a system of dispersed authority, where middle managers lead substantial areas of provision, and delegate further to leaders of operational teams. Lumby (2001, p. 22) argues that leadership in colleges is 'systemic', and refers to the image offered by Ogawa and Bossert (1997, p. 9) of leadership 'flowing' through the network of roles that characterize organizations.

For some, however, being a manager is seen in terms of 'taking the king's shilling' (Curriculum manager, College B), and to contemplate leadership is out of the question. Whatever the individual attitude of managers to leadership, they may be too constrained by operational activities and by the need for their actions to 'mesh' with others' for them to see themselves clearly as leaders. However, as Lumby (2001, p. 12) notes: 'leadership may be embodied in what people do, not what they say'. Evidence from the research suggests that middle managers, both individually and collectively, contribute to the whole leadership of the college.

Acceptance of leadership

Middle managers in the case-study colleges were cautious about the term 'leader'. They responded positively to the term 'lead teams and the individual', quoted from the occupational standards, perhaps because it echoed the familiar term 'team leader'. Some managers talked in terms of dispersed leadership, speaking of middle managers as 'experts in their own field or area', who developed their area of college provision on behalf of the senior management (Service manager, College A). Others related their role to aspects of transformational leadership:

> Your enthusiasm, your strategic thinking about the place – you're bringing people with you to make that happen. (Curriculum manager, College A)

For others, however, the term 'leader' was problematic. Having described her liaison role in relating the work of her team to that of the college, one manager commented:

> I shy away from describing myself as a leader ... I'm seen not as a leader, but as someone who works with [the team]. (Curriculum manager, College A)

This statement correlates with the position discussed in Chapter 5: leading the team while still being part of it. A curriculum manager at College C addressed the situation succinctly: 'I provide the lead, but I'm not a leader.'

Leadership is maintained through the trust, respect and authority given by the leader's team and colleagues, and there were strong positive instances of all three types of manager in this research having the trust, respect and authority by which to lead. A curriculum manager at College B emphasized that respect is necessary to support authority, and affirmed: 'I do feel that I have the authority, and people do listen to us.' Likewise, a student service manager at College D referred to the 'measure of respect' he needed from his colleagues: 'You have an instinctive feeling ... you know if you have that.' A service manager at College A talked of having 'the authority to persuade', and that 'you feel confident that most of the time you are trusted enough to be able to persuade'. All of these comments indicate that managers need both the collective authority given through their role and the individually given respect of one's colleagues in order to lead their area of provision.

On the other hand, middle managers can be reluctant to reconcile leadership with their own perception of their role: 'I would class myself as a facilitator, rather than a leader' (Curriculum manager, College C). Their own sense of authority is an influential factor. For example, a service manager at College C commented: 'Sometimes I feel as though I have enough authority and then sometimes I don't.' This uncertainty can be exacerbated through the attitude of senior managers: 'If something is going wrong, then you have the ton weight of senior management asking why' (Curriculum manager, College B). In none of these situations is the manager in a position to function as a leader: the first does not wish to lead, the second is uncertain as to who will follow, and the last may fear to lead. If leadership is, as Quinley *et al.* (1995) suggest, the action of using power to influence others in the accomplishment of important organizational objectives, these managers are, by their own assessment of the situation, not in a position to lead.

Reality check

What does leadership mean to you? Is it something that someone else does? Is it something which you enjoy doing, however well or badly you may do it?

Think through how you would carry out your role without using leadership skills. How would you carry out the other aspects of your role discussed so far – carrying out the purpose of the college, 'making it work' in your departmental area, managing staff, liaising with others – without the authority of leadership, and the power to influence others to achieve the essential work of the college?

What skills do you use in carrying out the above activities, which could reasonably be classed as 'leadership skills'? How

did you learn them, and what opportunities do you get to assess
and develop them further?

Do others accept you as leader? Are those who do mainly
your team members or your senior leaders? What does this
show about your position? Do some people not accept you as
leader: why not? Does this make your job more difficult?

Styles of leadership

In situations in which leadership was accepted by middle
managers in the case-study colleges, they favoured contingent
styles: styles chosen according to circumstance. The first reason
for this was expressed by a senior manager at College B, who
said: 'Your style has got to be something that really is your style,
not something you have read about in a book.' If leadership is a
state to which managers are reluctant to aspire, then the style
adopted has to suit their own personality and ways of interacting. Secondly, managers were perceptive in seeing that different leadership styles suit different followers: 'There are those
who need the functional and directional, and those who are far
happier with the transformational and the creative' (Service
manager, College C). As a senior manager at the same college
commented: 'one of the skills . . . is to decide when a particular
style is necessary'. Managers often work transactionally when
working with college systems, and transformationally when
enabling the work of their team. They attempt to 'blend' the
two, acknowledging that it is impossible to achieve the transactional without acting transformationally. As Glover *et al.*
(1999) conclude about subject leaders in schools, successful
departments occur when leaders recognize the difference
between the transactional and the transformational, and have
developed wisdom in handling personalities and situations. The
picture is built up, therefore, of managers having the capacity
and perception to use a range of leadership styles, within limits
in which they feel comfortable and in accordance with values
which they espouse, choosing according to circumstance the
style which will best produce the desired effect.

Reality check

Here in Figure 10 is a summary of the main styles of leadership which are commonly discussed and used.

Transactional	Organizational goals are carried out as a bargain – a transaction – based upon the individual interests of persons or groups. For example, the leader secures agreement for staff to carry out the functions of the organization in return for providing acceptable conditions of service and salary.
Directive	Similar to 'Transactional'. A managerial approach to leadership, based upon a hierarchy of command.
Instructional	(Not to be confused with directive!) Leadership based upon agreed educational values: those associated with teaching (i.e. instruction).
Transformational	Transformational leaders adopt a developmental role to influence the motives and values and goals of others in carrying out the vision of the organization, developing them, in turn, as leaders.
Distributed	In complex organizations, distributed leadership acts as a 'cascade effect' of transformational leadership, where followers are encouraged and influenced to set the pace and direction of their 'local' activity; leadership is accrued through successive layers of management.
Dispersed	Leadership is enacted at a 'local' level, but dispersed leadership may lack the whole-organization coherence of distributed systems.
Contingent	Contingent leaders choose their style according to context, depending upon the people or the task to be led. Response to context is the key factor which shapes their style in any given circumstance.

Figure 10 Styles of leadership

You may find different styles at work in different areas of the college leadership. For example, senior leaders at a college might use a transactional style, making it very clear what systems and operations they need the middle leaders to carry out. Some middle leaders might, in turn, act in ways that are transactional or directive – simply passing the orders on as contractual duties to be undertaken. Others might choose to share their leadership by distribution, passing on the leadership authority to others further 'down' the hierarchy, or they may work more closely with their team as transformational leaders, developing others' leadership skills.

You do not usually have the chance to choose what system you work within, but you have some choice of your own style. What style(s) do you tend to adopt, and why? Would another style work differently – or better?

Values, clarity and creativity

Leadership involves shaping and sharing values within the team, and middle managers in this study showed a strong concern for the educational values which underpinned their daily work with their teams.

> Teaching and learning, students' experience, trying to protect that and trying to enable staff to make a positive contribution to that. (Student service manager, College B)

> We have got a shared – is the word 'vision'? – with the kind of students we deal with and the kinds of experience we want them to have and it is pretty solid from the top to the bottom ... the students come first. (Curriculum manager, College D)

> No matter what we do around this table it's what we give to those kids out there and how we bring them on and make them better people in society, and that's what it's about. (Service manager, College B)

It is noticeable that the values of sustaining teaching and learning, and focusing on the primacy of the student learning experience, are consistent across the roles of the managers represented: for example, the last comment about bringing students on and making them 'better people in society' came from an estates manager.

A firm grasp of underlying values and purpose enables managers to be clear about their role, and as a senior manager at College B commented: 'If you are very clear about why you are there, and the importance of the staff you are working with, and what as a team you want to achieve, I believe you can be very effective.' Given that clarity of insight, some managers spoke with enthusiasm about shared vision within the team, setting the pace and direction of the team, and using their enthusiasm to bring people with them, being 'the person who has got to make sure that you get to where the strategic plan is leading you' (Service manager, College B).

Creative energy is important in leading these activities. Although creativity and innovation were constrained by time and working pressures, they were achieved by some, and aspired to by others:

> It's about being innovative. It is about being creative as to how those outcomes are to be achieved. (Service manager, College C)

> It is sometimes quite frustrating when you have particular ideas ... [for] curriculum development, and because of the restraints from other quarters within the college you're not able to do that. (Curriculum manager, College A)

This last comment underlines one of the major difficulties of 'leading from the middle' in a large and complex organization. Leadership is both shaped and constrained by the manager's multiple liaison with others. As one student service manager comments: 'We don't work in our nice little boxes ... there is a tension from other people in the organization whose targets you are affecting' (Student service manager, College A).

In three of the colleges, senior and middle managers spoke of college support for creativity and innovation. At College D, innovative leadership of new areas of provision was encouraged, with managers being seconded to develop and lead new initiatives. At College B, a senior manager observed that 'people here are encouraged to think out of boxes and develop and create', and considered that the non-hierarchical culture at the college enabled this. A student service manager at College C celebrated the culture at this newly established college of 'allowing people to be creative ... which means that some really good things have been developed', and a senior manager at the same college spoke of trying to 'nurture talent, spot talent'. Whether the creators and innovators saw themselves as leaders or not, these comments certainly indicate that there is an environment which encourages dispersed leadership at these colleges.

 Reality check

What values underpin the work that you do? How often, and in what ways, do you share them with your team?

Could the work of your team be more values-driven, or more creative? How would that change the way you work? Would it mean that you had to hand over some of your authority to others, or would it bring your team closer together?

Summary

College middle managers are reluctant to consider themselves as leaders. However, the managers in the case-study colleges undertook leadership activities such as shaping and sharing values within the team, 'bringing people with them' to make college functions happen, and setting the pace and direction of the team, all of which are activities noted by Sawbridge (2001) as important to leadership in further education. Leadership is, as Gronn (2000) observes, a phenomenon in the eye of the beholder, and middle managers show consistent evidence of leadership in the ways in which they enact their role, principally through their concern for values, for shaping the work of the department and enabling the work of their team. To a degree, they also encounter the respect, trust and authority which enable them to carry out a leadership role. They thus display three of the five structural relations described by Gronn (2000) as being significant features of dispersed leadership: authority, values and personal factors.

Leadership is enhanced when it conforms to the manager's value system, and the manager is able to relate to the underlying principles and practice of leadership within the working context. It is enabled by the manager's ability to understand and choose appropriate leadership styles according to context. It also depends upon whether the manager has the support of the college for creativity and innovation and the freedom and ability to set the pace and direction of the team.

Leadership is impeded by the managers' reluctance to acknowledge both the term and the concept as applied to themselves and their activities, a reluctance which may be induced by a lack of college acceptance of leadership in the context of middle management, and a lack of authority in role. Among the different types of manager role, the curriculum manager is most likely to experience conditions favourable to leadership. Service and student service managers, while they may enact leadership, are more likely to see themselves as 'team leaders' than as offering leadership for the college as a whole.

Modelling leadership

The leadership aspect of role is modelled in Figure 11. Leadership is strongly influenced by the attitudes of the middle managers themselves towards their own role, and the attitude of senior managers towards leadership. Managers may act as leaders without acknowledging it to themselves: in these cases leadership will not be carried out with any degree of focused reflection, and leadership skills may not be strongly developed. Leadership at middle-manager level is more likely to be acknowledged when senior managers lead transformationally and encourage distributed leadership, than within a transactional leadership environment.

Where the context for distributed leadership at the college is positive, and there is support for managers to take authority and to innovate, managers may develop their leadership roles in ways indicated in the model. They may feel that they have the authority to act creatively within their department, to set the pace and direction of their team, based upon values and purpose agreed within the team, and to distribute leadership appropriately to others. In these situations, the middle manager feels comfortable in accepting and developing their role as leader, and chooses styles which are appropriate to their context.

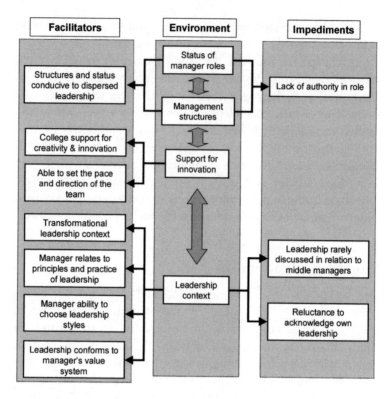

Figure 11 Modelling the leader aspect of role

Using the model

The model can be used to explore changing patterns of leadership at College A and College B. College A, at the time of the research visits, was moving towards a more distributed, transformational leadership style, in contrast to the transactional style which had been established over many years. This move showed confidence on the part of senior leaders that the college was securely established, and that leadership could therefore be distributed further. It was also related to the development of more dispersed, site-based management, which would hopefully ease the load of middle managers, and make them more effective. The middle managers at the college already showed awareness of a range of leadership styles and, that under the new system, managers might relate better to the principles and practice of leadership. However, their leadership might have to be developed upon a small existing base, as many of the facilitators in the model were missing. The transformational leadership context would take time to establish and be understood, and the accompanying encouragement for creativity and innovation would need to be fostered if the managers were to accept their new roles in a more transformational system.

In contrast, College B was moving from a transformational approach, based upon a common understanding of underpinning values, towards a more transactional approach, which offered better security for the college as a business. This move implies an increasingly insecure basis for distributed leadership. It may be that the strong directional leadership being developed to pull the college away from its various crises would be valued, and that the resulting loss of individual autonomy might be seen as a small price to pay for increased security. Once the college is secure, it may, like College A, revert to more distributed systems.

Contrary to the proposition of Burns and Stalker (1961), it appears from these examples that hierarchical, directive structures are favoured in times of turbulence, and organic, distributed structures are more likely to be adopted in times of greater stability. For the individual manager, turbulence within the college is likely to impede their already tenuous perception of their own position as leaders. Their focus is more likely to fall upon their other, more visible, aspects of role, and the leadership aspect may be the last to emerge within the new college environment.

Linking to the occupational standards

The main link to the occupational standards, is to the activities set out in Key Area C 'Lead teams and individuals' (Lifelong Learning UK 2005). The most relevant factors are to be found in the sub-sets 'Secure the respect, trust and support of colleagues, students and external contacts', and 'Contribute to the promotion and organisation of the sector.' Despite the closeness of the phrase 'secure the respect, trust and support of colleagues' to a number of factors discussed earlier in this chapter, the standards as a whole do not squarely address leadership as an issue. Leadership is seen more as a desirable trait in managing people and promoting the college than as a quality in itself. This may reflect the argument of this chapter that, although middle managers display leadership behaviours, they do not strongly see themselves as leaders.

This provokes the question: how would college cultures change if middle managers did see themselves more strongly as leaders? Individual areas of college provision might be developed more assertively and productively, but cross-college liaison, which is already difficult to achieve, might be made harder. The following set of questions may therefore be appropriate.

- In what circumstances do you see yourself as leader? What are the benefits of asserting your leadership position and adopting a proactive, creative stance towards your role in the college?
- Are there other circumstances in which asserting leadership would be beneficial? Would it enable you to secure the respect, support and trust of colleagues and students?
- Where does liaison get in the way of leadership? When is it more desirable professionally to adopt joint approaches with others? Is this simply a form of collaborative, shared leadership?
- On thinking through these issues, what do you think the college needs of you in terms of leadership?

This is the last of the separate aspects of the middle-manager role to be discussed in this book. The last two chapters move on to look at the role in its whole-college perspective, and to consider middle managers as professionals.

8 The whole-college context

So far, we have considered the various aspects of the manager's role separately. We have seen how managers in the case-study colleges view their role and, using the models based upon their experience, have discussed how contexts for the various middle-manager activities can be evaluated and strengthened. Breaking down a complex role into its constituent parts can help us to understand the forces and challenges at work. This chapter will move our thinking on to consider the whole middle-manager role within the whole college context. What, within the framework of the whole organization, helps managers to undertake their role successfully, and are all types of manager similarly affected by the whole-college context within which they work?

Modelling the whole-college context for management

The last model – Figure 12 – provides a complete picture of the middle-manager role and its interaction with the college as a whole; the various sets of facilitators and impediments in the previous models have been brought together to produce a single, overarching model. Around the centre are presented the main factors within the college which determine the middle-manager role: structures and territories; position; system design; role coherence and status; autonomy; and identification with leadership. Around the edge, we can see the sets of driving forces which shape those central factors. These offer us a means of interpreting pressures upon the middle-manager role, and of solving problems concerning college design and the ways in which managers interact.

This model offers a final distillation of the data from 16 senior managers, 45 middle managers and 288 team members, from observations of meetings and analysis of college documents at the four case-study colleges. The detail of the 'lived experience' of the middle managers and their role sets is lost, but the data from these college staff securely underpin what is presented here. Through representing their experience in this way, we can identify the underlying patterns and concepts which shape the daily lives of managers. In terms of Fowler

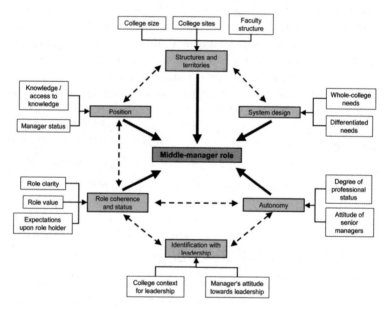

Figure 12 Modelling the middle-manager role within the college environment

(2003), the model in Figure 12 depicts the dynamic complexity of the colleges' management systems.

The inner set of factors presented in the model depicts the middle-manager role as being defined and circumscribed by the *college structures and territories* in which it is placed. The role is served, well or badly, by the *design of the systems* in operation at the college, and by the *manager's position* in relation to understanding the college as a whole. The role is also defined by the expectations of members of the role set, and by the value which they place upon the role: factors which govern the *coherence and status* of the role. Finally, it is influenced by the *degree of autonomy* and the extent and the *nature of leadership* which the role-holder experiences. These six concepts interlink as a system; however, we will first consider how each one relates to the manager role.

The *structures and territories* are the physical structures – the college's buildings and sites – and the management-based structures of the college – the faculties and departments. Within those structures are the managers' territories. Territories are beneficial, offering a physical or work-based location within the college with which people can identify and feel 'at home', and within which the links between people are strong. They can also present barriers to people from other territories, who may not understand the systems and values at work, or who may simply be unwelcome. The operation of these structures and territories can present tension between whole-organizational systems and individual or group working.

Position represents not only the managers' location within the management structure, but also their placing in respect to understanding whole-college issues. Favourable position may offer the manager access to both knowledge and status; it may also be given as a 'reward' to those who have knowledge and status. Knowledge in this context is professional knowledge, as discussed by Turner and Bolam (1998), particularly the manager's understanding of the further education context, the college and how it works, and knowledge of educational practice within their particular field. So, professional knowledge is a key to securing position, and position offers access to increased knowledge.

System design considers the efficiency and effectiveness of the college's operational systems. Ideally, the overall system design should offer the best possible help to all users, and its constituent parts. For example, the individual college systems for quality control or for managing finance should operate in synchrony with each other. Given the size of FE colleges, and their diversity of operation, this 'ideal' presents difficulties: of overall system design (given that different parts of the system are usually designed by different people), of people's understanding of the design, and of cooperation to achieve synchrony between the parts. There is also tension between systems which are predominantly mechanical, serving the corporate needs of the whole organization, and those which are organic, differentiated to the needs of sub-sections of the organization. In order to meet the diverse needs of the total system, and to survive, the organization has to maintain a balance between them.

Role coherence and status is made up of the expectations upon the manager, how clear their role is to the role set and the extent to which the manager and their role are valued. If their received role is clear, the possibility is increased of avoiding role ambiguity, role overload and sent role conflict. Status is often given to the role itself, regardless of who holds it, but can also be awarded to the role-holder personally, in recognition of their professional knowledge and skills.

Autonomy sums up the extent to which managers are free to interpret and carry out their role, within an understanding of whole-college purpose. It is partly determined by the attitude of senior managers towards the middle-manager role, and is linked with the degree of professional status perceived by the manager. Gleeson and Shain (1999) consider that a loss of professional autonomy has been experienced in FE colleges through management reorganization. Autonomy is felt to be under pressure, constrained by the bureaucratic needs of the whole organization.

Identification with leadership assesses whether the manager is psychologically and positionally ready for leadership. It depends upon the manager accepting that the concept of leadership applies to them, and upon whether the prevailing leadership styles of the college encourage distributed leadership. Identification with leadership is more likely to occur in transformational leadership contexts than transactional.

All of these factors are interdependent, as suggested by the dashed arrows in the model. The top three elements are closely interlinked: college operational and implementation systems usually flow along the framework provided by the college structures. The manager's position is partly determined by the college structures, but also by the status of the role and the manager's acceptability within the dominant college territories. The lower set of elements is likewise interlinked, and is strongly dependent upon people's attitudes and perceptions. The case-study managers did not identify strongly with leadership, so this factor has no direct line of impact upon the centre of the model. The managers' identification with leadership is more likely to be linked to their status as managers or to the degree of autonomy which they experience than to any personal need to be seen as leaders.

 ## Reality check

The six areas discussed above are of key importance to middle managers if they are to carry out their role effectively. Look back at them, and consider what they mean to you in your situation. Think about each of them, and consider whether you are in a strong position in relation to each of them. For example, do the structures and territories of the college give you security and support you in your role, or do they get in the way of your liaison with others? Do the college systems seem

	Strong position	Weak position	Action
College structures and territories			
Position within the college			
Design of college systems			
Role coherence and status			
Autonomy of own role			
Identification with leadership			

Figure 13 Assessing your position

designed to help you or to hinder you? Do you identify strongly with the idea of being a leader?

You will find that the Figure 13 is over-simplistic. Inevitably, you will wish to 'tick both boxes', as, for example, your role may be coherent on some days but not others, or it may be coherent, but lack status. It is the thinking which is stimulated as you decide where to tick that is important, not how many ticks result.

Similarly, the 'action' boxes are far too small. This is deliberate. Wherever you feel you are in a 'weak position', try to think of one thing which you can do to address the situation. Remember, you cannot change the whole college yourself – think of one thing which *you* can do, to make your position more secure.

Then look through your set of action points, and see whether there is any way in which you can address them together: it is easier to have one coherent aim than six disjointed ones. For example, if you are a service manager, you could decide to set up a working party to enable the systems which you run to work better throughout the college. This would:

a) give you a mandate to work across the college structures and territories
b) enhance your own position within the college through more people being aware of your knowledge and expertise
c) improve the design of the systems which you run
d) make your role clearer to others in the college, and influence others' expectations of you
e) enable you to demonstrate creativity and decision-making through the way you carry out your role
f) enable you to see yourself more clearly as leader.

Using the model

Let us take real-life examples, based on the case-study colleges, of questions raised by each cluster of factors. To take the element – structures and territories – Colleges A and C which operate on multiple sites were striving to find the optimum structure for operating across sites, but Colleges B and D, which are strongly faculty-based, appeared less concerned about the territorial barriers which their structures present. Presumably Colleges B and D value their strong faculty systems – but are they fully aware of the difficulties which their systems present for managers who work across faculties?

Secondly, considering system design, managers who design college operational and implementation systems may keep in mind the whole-college needs which the systems serve, but may give less consideration to the differentiated needs of the various sections of the college. At its extreme, this could result in a system of whole-college simplicity which is unworkable on a departmental basis. It may be impossible to balance whole-college needs with all of the needs of the different departments, but the model serves as a reminder that both sets of needs must be borne in mind.

Thirdly, reflecting on 'position', managers new to role could be encouraged to analyse their position, perhaps with a view to strengthening it. What professional knowledge and expertise do they bring to the role, and how well are they placed to learn more about the college and its purpose? How well known and well regarded is their knowledge, and how does it support their status within the college?

This leads on to the fourth element, 'role coherence and status': most of the managers in this study experienced some degree of role strain, which could have been due to conflicting – or excessive – expectations upon them. Middle managers and their senior leaders might usefully discuss the range of expectations upon the middle managers, in order to define the role more clearly and realistically. This should lead to the identification and alleviation of 'pressure points' for role conflict, ambiguity and overload.

Fifthly, in at least one college in the present study (College A) senior managers would have liked middle managers to have more autonomy in role. The model indicates that they should consider the degree of professional status accorded to the role-holders, and examine their own attitude towards the day-to-day reality of middle-manager autonomy. The discussion on autonomy in the 'reality check' below offers a useful starting point.

Finally, senior managers at College C wished for more dispersed leadership within the college: their staff-development programme might therefore usefully include an examination of the college context for leadership, and of the managers' attitude towards leadership, in order to strengthen college-wide identification with the concept.

Reality check

These six examples give some indication of how we can use parts of the model to examine the 'health' of the whole system. Let us look at issues raised by two of the clusters in more detail.

College systems

This cluster highlights the tension which exists both for system-makers and system-users: college systems must serve both the needs of the college as a whole and the differentiated needs of its departments. System-makers and system-users need therefore to be in constant dialogue, to avoid the tactics of imposition on the one hand and of non-compliance on the other. Managers must appreciate the difficulty of meeting both whole-college and departmental needs, and work together for the best possible solution. As the majority of both system-makers and system-users are likely to be middle managers, this is one understanding which lies at the heart of both college effectiveness and the effectiveness of the individual manager.

Middle-manager autonomy

One issue discussed in the case studies by both senior and middle managers was the level of autonomy needed by the middle managers in order to carry out their role effectively. Some senior leaders wished that their middle managers would 'seize' more autonomy, and take greater responsibility for their role; some middle managers (mainly college service managers) saw their role as being to serve the system rather than as acting autonomously; other middle managers (mainly curriculum managers) felt that they needed autonomy to support their professional status.

The factors linked in the model with autonomy suggest questions such as the following.

- Does this role have particular professional status: is this middle manager the college 'expert' in a particular field?
- Do senior managers feel that it is appropriate, in a whole-college context, to devolve responsibility to this manager?
- Do either the senior managers or the middle manager see this role in terms of dispersed leadership?
- Does the college need and expect the manager to act autonomously to a significant extent?

Through questioning such as this, the levels of autonomy needed within a particular college setting can be understood. Changes can be assessed. For example, if a particular manager were given greater autonomy, then:

1. The status of the role and of the manager personally would be increased.
2. There would be greater devolved responsibility upon the manager.
3. The relationship of the manager with senior managers would change.
4. The manager might be more encouraged to adopt a leadership role.
5. The college might make better use of the manager's expertise.

This set of factors in turn raises questions about whether the manager, their role set and the college are capable and willing to act within this changed situation. It enables the situation to be assessed before it actually takes place – and may indeed prevent it from taking place. In this way, the model can be used to predict what would happen if various elements in the model were strengthened, diminished or removed; this activity thus enables a process of strategic decision-making.

Effects of college turbulence

Any analysis of the whole-college system would have to take account of turbulence. Turbulence can be produced by external or internal factors, but there is often a combination of the two, as the college responds internally to an external impact. Data from this study suggest that turbulence affects all aspects of the manager role; however, it is possible that some elements of the college system may be more strongly affected than others. This statement can best be analysed by comparing the situation at Colleges B and C, as these colleges were experiencing both externally and internally induced turbulence at the time of the research. College B was adjusting its management style after a series of crises, including a disappointing inspection and loss of staff through financial instability; College C was stabilizing its structures and systems after a complex amalgamation process and attempting rapid change in order to respond to local and national initiatives. At College C, the turbulence affected mainly the top three elements of the model in Figure 12. The structures were constantly under adjustment, and managers expressed frustration with cumbersome college systems; however, the college's purpose and values were well understood, thus strengthening the top portion of the model.

At College B, in contrast, there was significant uncertainty about the whole-college values and purpose; these aspects had seemed clear before the crises, and were subsequently less clear. At this college, the lower elements of the model had been destabilized; there was both role ambiguity owing to the move towards more managerial systems, and role overload as a result of loss of staff. Autonomy, which had previously been valued, had been put in question, and the environment for leadership was uncertain. The college was concentrating on strengthening its systems and structures; hopefully this would produce conditions of greater stability.

From these two examples it appears that turbulence does not always affect the same parts of the system; the models can therefore be used to identify where the turbulence has most impact, and what the compensating factors might be. The model could thus be used as a tool for managing externally or internally generated change, through a consideration of scenarios which would be produced by the change and an analysis of how to mediate the anticipated turbulence.

Differences between managers

Throughout this book, we have discussed managers holding different roles together, as the collective middle management of the college. This is because, in whole-college terms, they carry out the same types of activity, such as implementation, staff management and liaison. However, from discussion in this chapter, it can be seen that some managers are better placed to carry out their work than others. The section below sets out the main differences between managers in carrying out their work, as demonstrated at the case-study colleges.

Curriculum managers

On the whole, curriculum managers are well placed within the college structure. They are seen – by themselves and others – as carrying out the purpose of the college through their management of teaching and learning. College structures therefore tend to be built around them. The comparative insularity offered by the college structure may, however, prevent them from interacting easily with other managers, and even from understanding whole-college values and purpose.

Curriculum managers do not generally create college systems. Logically, the systems should be designed to help the college enact its purpose, and curriculum managers should therefore benefit, but this is not always the case. If liaison is poor, particularly between the service managers who devise and operate the systems and the curriculum managers who use them, the work of both will be impaired.

Curriculum manager roles are generally valued, for the reasons given above. Role ambiguity can be experienced, however, especially between curriculum managers and student service managers. Close cooperation is needed between these two sets of managers over provision for students, and sometimes the roles overlap, causing ambiguity. Given their status in leading an area of the college curriculum, curriculum managers generally have scope for creativity and interpretation in their role, and they value this factor as part of their professionalism. They may, reluctantly, see themselves as leaders.

On the above analysis, it appears that curriculum managers are well supported by many of the factors set out in the final model. Their effectiveness, and through them the effectiveness of the college, depends on how well they understand the whole-college purpose and values, and how well they liaise with other managers who are crucial to their success.

Student service managers

Student service managers need access to all the structures and territories of the college in order to manage their dispersed staff and to liaise over student provision. They are therefore most likely of all the managers to experience difficulty with college structures and territories, which tend to be curriculum- or site-based rather than service-based. Student service managers create some of the college systems, however, which gives them a certain amount of security, and the broad-ranging nature of their role usually places them in a position to understand whole-college values and purpose.

Student service managers have to be responsive to individual and collective student need, and they therefore usually have scope for case-by-case interpretation and creativity in their role. Student service roles may not be understood or valued in themselves, however: it is the effective manager him- or herself who is valued. Respect has to be earned from other managers and staff through the quality of service offered to students. Student service managers may see themselves as team leaders, but their role probably depends too much on liaison for them to see themselves in conventional leadership terms. From this analysis, it appears that there are both strengths and difficulties built into this role. It is not a role which has automatic status, yet it covers such fundamental college activities as enrolling students, providing them with computer systems and learning resources and supporting their individual needs. The role therefore contributes to whole-college effectiveness through serving the needs of the differentiated parts of the system.

Service managers

Service managers are responsible for what are seen as the 'managerial' aspects of college life. They create college systems and implement national ones – for example for handling finance and management information, human resource management and managing estates. Some of these systems, notably finance and management information, link the college with its funding bodies, and some govern key internal functions, such as the employment of staff at the college. Potentially, therefore, this situation offers status to service managers. Interview data suggest that service managers have a good understanding of whole-college purpose and values, and wish to liaise effectively with other managers. However, they are not well placed to work across college territories, and are often placed in a separate strand of the management structure: interaction with other managers to achieve mutual understanding can therefore be difficult.

Service managers on the whole do not wish for autonomy, although they are often involved in creating systems. Their function is to manage systems, and to operate them efficiently. Although they potentially have status, their roles are not always well understood, and their nature means that they are associated negatively with college bureaucracy. Like the student service managers, therefore, they have to earn respect in their role in order to be valued.

The coherent college

The discussion in this chapter so far demonstrates the complexity of colleges as organizations, and hence the difficulty of achieving coherent management systems. So what would a coherent college look like? It was argued in Chapter 2 that, in order to manage the range of provision which is needed for students, colleges allocate functions to a network of departments and managers. For the student to have a successful educational experience, this complex web of provision has to work as a coherent whole.

No two 'coherent' colleges would be identical: the discussion above about turbulence indicates that colleges have different strengths and vulnerabilities, just as they have different numbers of sites and demonstrate different patterns of leadership. This discussion acknowledges such difference, while offering insight into generic enabling features.

First, in a coherent college, the structures and territories would be easy to work across. College hierarchies and structures tend to be 'vertical', based on blocks of provision within a faculty or on a site. This makes it difficult for managers to work laterally, establishing working relationships across the various parts of college provision. A coherent college would have established ways of enabling lateral, as well as vertical, interaction.

Secondly, the college systems would facilitate both efficiency and effectiveness. With constraints upon funding, and high levels of political accountability, colleges have no choice but to be efficient, and in the coherent college this efficiency would result in operational systems which were well designed for their purpose, and quick and easy to use. The systems are also judged by how effectively they enable the college to meet its professional accountability and meet the needs of the market, through providing appropriate learning opportunities for students and clients. This demands a degree of 'local' flexibility, in order to respond effectively to individual circumstance. It is important to review and redesign systems on a regular basis, in order to keep them fit for both purposes.

Thirdly, managers would be well placed to understand whole-college values and purpose; they would use that understanding to apply their professional knowledge appropriately, both in their departments and in contributing to whole-college decision-making. This study shows inconsistency in middle managers' understanding of, and participation in, whole-college issues. If the college, as a complex multi-structured organization, is to function coherently, then the managers of the individual 'segments' of activity have to be in a position to understand and relate to whole-college purposes and values, in order to enact them appropriately within their departments.

The fourth element in whole-college coherence is that manager roles would be understood and valued. This entails an acknowledgement of the status of all types of manager in contributing to the whole-college operation. There is an indication that attitudes towards manager roles may be changing, with 'service' staff acquiring status through acknowledgement of their professional expertise, but this change is not complete. Also, the negative effects of role conflict, role ambiguity and role overload seem to pervade both the data in this study and the middle-manager literature. In this situation, managers may 'retreat' to an operational or managerial function when they are overloaded in order to minimize the demands upon them.

Fifthly, this research indicates that whole-college coherence is supported where managers have a degree of autonomy, giving them scope for interpretation and creativity in their role. The multiple functions of the college depend upon 'local' specialist expertise. If managers feel that their autonomy and creativity are unduly restricted in the very area in which their expertise lies, both their motivation and their ability to manage will be restricted.

The last element of whole-college coherence concerns distributed leadership. If 'being a leader' conforms to the managers' value systems, then their professional identity may include a leadership role. If leadership is distributed, it is a joint, communal activity aimed at a common purpose; this understanding would enable whole-college and departmental function to be harmonized. A system of dispersed leadership, encouraged by transformational leadership at senior level, would also strengthen the middle-manager role as 'local expert'. Neither the literature on FE colleges, nor the evidence from this research indicate that distributed leadership of this kind is consciously in operation to any significant extent.

As the Foster Report (Foster 2005) points out, there is a lack of coherence of college systems, data handling and management practice across the FE sector. Constructing the 'coherent college' has to be undertaken in response to local factors, as each college has a unique context, and different strengths and points of vulnerability. It also has to be undertaken in response to national initiatives to improve and rationalize the work of the sector. If the sector is to shed its reputation as a 'disadvantaged middle child' between schools and higher education (Foster 2005, p. 7), the concept of professionalism, discussed in the final chapter must come to the fore.

9 The 'new professionals'

In the previous chapter we looked at the middle manager's role within its college environment: how managers holding different responsibilities function within the whole-college setting. This final chapter offers an assessment of the middle-manager role itself, through considering middle managers as professionals. As the Foster Report (Foster 2005, p. 10) asserts:

> We need an FE college system — not sector — for the future which ... has a purposeful, skilled, professional and inspiring workforce.

Changing professionalism?

If we are to understand fully the work of FE managers, and strengthen their role in colleges, it is important to define their profession. To what profession do they belong? The incorporation of colleges in 1992, which was discussed in Chapter 1, brought fundamental changes for those working in the sector. Incorporation brought new forms of governance for colleges, and colleges became responsible for important areas of management such as finance, estates and human resource management. During the 1990s there was also a new government focus on strategic planning and the financial 'health' of colleges, together with new inspection and self-assessment regimes. These two sets of changes — increased levels of college autonomy together with heightened accountability — fundamentally altered the role of college managers at senior and middle levels, and produced tensions within the sector.

Chapter 1 described the turbulence in the college sector in the 1990s, with industrial conflict over lecturer contracts and staff redundancies. There were concerns about the growth of managerialism, which, according to Randle and Brady (1997), clashed with the value system of academic staff, whose 'professionalism' focused upon student learning, a concern for academic standards and professional autonomy. Since 1997 other researchers (for example, Gleeson and Shain 1999) have questioned the premise of a pre-incorporation 'golden age' of professional learner-centred activity in colleges.

Research by Lumby and Tomlinson (2000) and by Simkins (2000) shows evidence of an acceptance of the realities of college accountability and indicates the coexistence of both managerial and professional approaches: the notion begins to take shape that 'being a professional' may well include undertaking managerial activities. Gleeson (2001) takes this debate further. He writes of the 're-professionalisation' of FE, which might be seen as adopting a new, businesslike approach to the 'old' values of addressing the learning needs of students. This approach is not uniform across colleges: a related paper by Gleeson and Shain (1999, p. 467) discusses the 'struggle over the meaning and identity of professionals' in FE colleges, indicating that the 'profession' of college managers is not yet agreed and established.

Professionalism in colleges is related to the public-sector values of service to the community, together with a pedagogical concern for the individual learner. This is a professionalism to which curriculum managers, and other managers within colleges, might subscribe. This kind of professionalism appears to be set in tension with the need to apply business practices to the provision of education. How can learning be a business? This is the dilemma which has been at the heart of the debate.

Changes in the operational management of colleges have introduced other concepts of professionalism into the picture. At incorporation, many colleges appointed academic members of staff to lead the new 'service' departments such as finance, human resources and student services, but during the 1990s these roles were increasingly allocated to specialist professionals, with qualifications in accountancy, personnel management or the management of services to students. This trend coincided with the height of the industrial unrest in colleges, and, due to the nature of their roles, these managers tend to be associated negatively with 'managerialist' values (Gleeson 2001). Potentially, therefore, there was a clash of professional identities between service managers and those managing the curriculum.

However, given the need to apply businesslike principles to performing the educational purpose of the college, it was necessary for these professional identities to be reconciled in order for the college to succeed. The research which underpins this book took place ten years after incorporation, and offers some insight into the development of 'new professional' roles for college managers. If colleges are to respond to the Foster Report (Foster 2005, p. 11) they must 'have committed and professional teachers, trainers and support staff who are proud to work in FE'. Managers interviewed for the research were certainly 'proud to work in FE', and demonstrated understanding of their emerging professional identities.

Exploring professionalism

Professionalism could be defined as the espousal of a set of values or codes, which we consciously 'profess' and monitor through our individual reflection or through organizational systems. As we saw in Chapter 4, managers holding different types of role in College A gave insight into how their professionalism operated.

> One of the most important things to do as a manager is to *carve out the space*, define it, know it well. (Service manager)

> We all of us have different *professional standards*. I know what a library should be like in terms of how it looks, the stock, how the stock should interact with users. (Student service manager)

> There is a certain amount of *respect* now for the ability of heads of school to determine what the curriculum should be. ... There are, if you like, very broad strategies or targets set up, and how you make it happen is up to you. (Curriculum manager)

These speakers indicate that a professional manager must know what the role entails, have the specialist knowledge to enable it to be carried out, and earn respect from others through the way in which it is performed.

Knowing what the role entails is achieved in different ways. As was seen in Chapter 4, for the managers' team members, professionalism meant the 'smooth running' of departmental operations: managing learning resources; finance; space and staff (Student service team member, College A); booking rooms; planning programmes; attending meetings; and balancing budgets (Curriculum team member, College B).

The specialist knowledge could be, for a student service manager, 'funding changes, new legislation … government changes to benefit law' (College A). For a curriculum manager, it might be new developments within their subject discipline, but it could equally be 'all the links I've got with vocational teams, about how to make the curriculum work in that particular area' (College C): the professional knowledge here is in the *application* of the curriculum. Similarly, an estates manager spoke of the liaison which was necessary in order to interpret curriculum need in terms of accommodation and IT provision, emphasizing that 'the dialogue between middle managers … is crucial' (College B). These examples indicate that specialist knowledge needs to be acquired, applied and shared in order for these managers to carry out their roles.

Respect for the professional in carrying out their role is more problematic. There are power differentials between the different types of manager surveyed, and on the whole, curriculum managers hold most power through being perceived as 'nearest' to student learning, which is the purpose of the college. There are signs, however, of perceptions changing, and of all roles being seen as sharing the common purpose of supporting learning. Mutual understanding of this shared purpose may lead to greater equality for the various manager roles, and a clearer understanding of, and respect for, each other's professional performance.

Differing 'professionalisms'?

The middle managers whose roles were analysed during the research – curriculum managers, managers of services to students, and heads of college services – may be seen as sharing common values, but having potentially different bases for their professionalism. The differences between middle-manager roles which were noted in Chapter 8 are important elements of this debate.

On the whole, curriculum managers are seen as enacting the purpose of the college through their management of teaching and learning, and this is the basis of their professionalism. However, their profession may be to 'be an engineer', rather than to 'manage engineering provision'. Their professional identity may lie in what they provide, rather than how they provide it. Their professional role as college managers may also be restricted, depending upon the extent of their whole-college understanding, and how well they liaise with other managers to ensure effective learning across the college.

The professionalism of student service managers lies in the extent to which they can provide a range of services to students across the whole spectrum of college provision. The broad-ranging nature of their role usually places them in a position to understand whole-college values and purpose, and to relate their own professional function to the needs of the college. They need access to all parts of the college in order to manage staff who are widely dispersed, and to liaise with other managers over student provision. Their professional role depends to a large extent on the success of their liaison with others to provide for student need.

Service managers create college systems and implement national ones – that is their profession. Some systems, notably finance and management information, link the college with its funding bodies, and some govern key internal functions, such as the employment of staff at the college; potentially this situation offers a 'ready-made' professionalism. However, these managers can also be associated negatively with college bureaucracy. Like the student service managers, therefore, they have to earn respect in role in order to be valued: their professionalism needs to be understood and drawn upon by other managers.

Interview data suggested that service managers have a good understanding of whole-college purpose and values, and wish to liaise effectively with other managers. However, they are not well placed to work across college structures and territories, often being placed in a separate structure of their own, and interaction with other managers can be difficult. This in turn impedes the respect they may earn from other managers, which can result in service managers being the target of 'blame cultures', and in their professionalism being poorly understood.

A senior manager at College B illustrated the development of understanding of professionalism at his college:

> What colleges have had to do ... is realise that we needed to professionalize some of the services that we offer, like finance, like human resources, like estates.

He spoke of previous customary practice, where a 'semi-redundant head of department' would have been 'converted' into these roles, and commented that this was an unprofessional approach to managing the college. He then added:

> Maybe there is the same lesson to be learned about the way in which we organise the administration for the college in order to service the needs of students and the needs of the teaching departments.

What he aspired to was the professional leadership and management of curriculum areas and services to students, in line with the professional approach already adopted in the college service areas. These comments match the observations by Gleeson and Shain (1999) and Gleeson (2001) that the new professionalism in colleges encompasses the notion of being 'businesslike', alongside a concentration on its 'business', which is satisfying the learning needs of students.

Reality check

Your professionalism is based upon three linked elements:

- Professional values: what I profess.
- Professional identity: the profession to which I belong.
- Professional role: my role within the whole-college setting.

Note down for yourself your responses to these three elements. What do you profess? What is the profession to which you belong? What is your professional role within the college setting?

Share your responses with other middle managers. What do you have in common? Where do you differ? Do the differences matter? Do they affect the way you work with each other? What do you need to understand about each other in order to work well together?

Achieving professionalism

The research undertaken for this book indicates that if professionalism is to be achieved, each college will seek its own definition, based upon an agreed understanding of the educational values of the college, what its purpose is in relation to its clients and students, and how this purpose is to be achieved. The external pressures both for business efficiency and for effective, meaningful outcomes for clients are strong and, through its own unique combination of internal and external factors, each college will come to its own point of balance.

The research has shown that in colleges there is only a partial understanding of how the different sections of the college operate, how they fit together, and how they can work together to reach clients and to provide learning for them. What this indicates is that there is not only a need to understand professionalism, but also a need for professionalism to be shared throughout the organization: if one section of the college defines it differently from another (as at present they probably do), then the college will not operate coherently. In particular, management can no longer be purely an intuitive, instinctive activity, undertaken within the rush and bustle of college life.

Managers should be encouraged and enabled to develop their management skills, to share with each other their understanding of the issues, values and principles underpinning the work of the college operation, and to understand and value each other's professional work.

There are indications from the research that both middle and senior managers are striving to create a middle-manager role which takes account of whole-college purpose and values, and the businesslike management of education within the college sector, and makes full use of the 'local' knowledge, expertise and specialisms within the college departments. Developing 'professionalized' management involves cross-college discussion of the fitness-for-purpose of college structures and systems, and of the scope of individual manager roles. Shared professionalism entails not only an awareness of what management is, but also of what it does: what managers can jointly achieve in terms of outcomes for clients and students. This 'new professionalism' is not yet in place, but is aspired to, and would constitute a successful balance for the manager between meeting the corporate needs of the college and the individual learning needs of clients and students, resolving the difficult equation of business with learning.

 ## Reality check

In the 'reality check' sections of the previous chapters, the following issues have been raised.

Use the list in Figure 14 to identify where your own development needs are. Reread the section preceding a 'reality check' that is important for you, to understand the issues and to relate them to your own work. Look again at the model for that chapter. See where your issue fits in the model, what factors are related to it, and think about how you can address them. Liaise with your staff development officer to plan development which will address that issue for yourself and others.

Chapter	Issue	Page
2	College structures	19
	The pressures and dilemmas of 'managing in the middle'	21
3	Understanding whole-college issues	31
	Bureaucracy and accountability	33
4	Working with college systems	42
	Reporting and supplying data	44
	Your budget	45
	Managing overload	48
	Expertise and professionalism	49
5	Managing the individual, the team and the task	59
	Managing people	62
	Managing people at a distance	64
	Managing from the middle	66
	Managing difficult staff	67
6	Being 'piggy in the middle'	76
	Liaising across the college	78
	Support from senior managers	80
	Issues of status and territory	82
7	What does leadership mean to you?	89
	Leadership styles	91
	Understanding your values	94
8	Your role within the whole-college context	103
	Examine the health of the system	106
9	Understanding your professionalism	121

Figure 14 'Reality check' sections

The challenge of middle management

The elements in the table above emphasize the huge range of the middle-manager role, and the problems and challenges which the role brings with it. They also underline the fact that being a manager in an FE college *is* a profession, however that may be defined. The central chapters in the book set out the key aspects of the middle-manager role: managing the college, 'making it happen', managing people, working together, leadership. These are activities which managers often carry out intuitively, learning 'on the job', or through observing others. Yet they are hugely important to the work of the college, and to the sector. The national workforce development strategy proposed by the Foster Report calls for a clear plan for improving leadership and management across the sector: 'Strong and effective management and leadership makes a critical difference to quality and impact' (Foster 2005, p. 74). The management activities discussed here – and the skills which underpin them – need to be focused upon and evaluated by the manager, the college and the sector as a whole.

In the Introduction, I explained that this is not a book which will 'give you the answers' and tell you 'how to manage'. How could it? No two roles and no two colleges are alike. What is offered here are ways of thinking about your role, understanding it through the eyes and voices of others, and seeing how you can develop your skills in your role further. Through reading about the difficulties of, for example, managing people, you learn that you are not alone, that the task *is* difficult, not because of your lack of ability, but because of the complexity of people and how they interact. This should encourage you to discuss management problems more freely with others, and to seek joint approaches to common situations.

The sets of questions and thinking tools offered in the 'reality checks' can form the basis of staff-development sessions. Equally, they may provide you with issues to read further about. Most college libraries provide a good starting-point, and organizations such as the Quality Improvement Agency and the Centre for Excellence in Leadership offer access both to further reading and to programmes of development. You may become involved in research within your college, to find out more about 'how it works' and how its working can be improved.

The models in each of the central chapters of this book provide ways of understanding influences on the middle-manager role, which can be explored collectively by middle and senior managers to identify and address problems, and make the work of middle management run more smoothly. As they derive from research into middle management, they could also form a useful starting point for further research. You could take a cluster of elements from a model which interests you and investigate how it works in your college. For the college to succeed, middle managers need to be engaged in management issues, inquisitive about their work, aware of their own and others' roles in managing the college. As a result, they will work together professionally to meet the needs and purposes of the college, its learners and its clients.

References

Adair, J. (1983) *Effective Leadership*, London: Pan.

Ainley, P. and Bailey, B. (1997) *The Business of Learning*, London: Cassell.

Alexiadou, N. (2001) 'Management identities in transition: a case study from further education', *The Sociological Review*, 49 (3), pp. 412–35.

Bennett, N. (1995) *Managing Professional Teachers: Middle managers in primary and secondary schools*, London: Paul Chapman.

Bolton, A. (2000) *Managing the Academic Unit*, Milton Keynes: Society for Research into Higher Education/Open University Press.

Brown, M. and Rutherford, D. (1998) 'Changing roles and raising standards: New challenges for heads of department', *School Leadership and Management*, 18 (1), pp. 75–88.

Bureaucracy Review Group for Further Education and Training (2004) *Annual Report 2004*, London: DfES.

Burnham, P. (1969) 'Role theory and educational administration', in G. Baron and W. Taylor (eds) *Educational Administration and the Social Sciences*, London: Athlone Press.

Burns, T. and Stalker, G. M. (1961) *The Management of Innovation*, London: Tavistock Publications.

Centre for Excellence in Leadership (2005) *Whatever Happened to the War on Bureaucracy?* London: CEL.

Department for Education and Skills (2002) *Success for All: Reforming further education and training*, London: DfES.

Drodge, S. (2002) 'Managing under pressure: The management of vocational education in the British, Dutch and French systems', *Research in Post-compulsory Education*, 7 (1), pp. 27–43.

Elliott, G. (2000) 'Accrediting lecturers using competence-based approaches: A cautionary tale', in D. Gray and C. Griffin (eds) *Post-compulsory Education and Training for the New Millennium*, London: Jessica Kingsley.

Foster, A. (2005) *Realising the Potential: a review of the Future Role of Further Education Colleges*, London: DfES.

Fowler, A. (2003) 'Systems modelling, simulation, and the dynamics of strategy', *Journal of Business Research*, 56, pp. 135–44.

Further Education National Training Organisation (2001) *National Occupational Standards for Management in Further Education*, London: FENTO.

Gillett-Karam, R. (1999) 'Midlevel management in the community college: a rose garden?' in R. Gillett-Karam (ed.) *Preparing Departmental Chairs for their Leadership Roles*, San Francisco: Jossey-Bass.

Gleeson, D. (2001) 'Style and substance in education leadership; Further education (FE) as a case in point', *Journal of Educational Policy*, 16 (3), pp. 181–96.

Gleeson, D. and Shain, F. (1999) 'Managing ambiguity: Between markets and managerialism – a case study of "middle" managers in further education', *The Sociological Review*, 47 (3), pp. 461–90.

Glover, D. and Miller, D. with Gambling, M., Gough, G. and Johnson, M. (1999) 'As others see us: Senior management and subject staff perceptions of the work effectiveness of subject leaders in secondary schools', *School Leadership and Management*, 19 (3), pp. 331–44.

Goode, W. J. (1960) 'A theory of role strain', *American Sociological Review*, 25, pp. 161–8.

Gronn, P. (2000) 'Distributed properties: a new architecture for leadership', paper presented at BEMAS Research 2000, Cambridge, 29–31 March.

Hammons, J. (1984) 'The department/division chairperson: educational leader?', *Community and Junior College Journal*, March.

Hewitt, P. and Crawford, M. (1997) 'Introducing new contracts: Managing change in the context of an enterprise culture', in R. Levacic and R. Glatter (eds) *Managing Change in Further Education*, FEDA Report, 1 (7), London: Further Education Development Agency.

Howell, J. M. and Hall-Meranda, K. E. (1999) 'The ties that bind: the impact of leader–member exchange, transformational and transactional leadership, and distance on predicting follower performance', *Journal of Applied Psychology*, 84 (5), pp. 680–94.

Jackson, J. A. (1972) *Role*, Cambridge: Cambridge University Press.

Kahn, R. L., Wolfe, D. M., Quinn, R. P., Snoek, J. D. with Rosenthal, R. A. (1964) *Organizational Stress: Studies in role conflict and ambiguity*, New York: John Wiley and Sons.

Katz, D. and Kahn, R. L. (1966) *The social psychology of organizations*, New York: John Wiley.

Learning and Skills Council (2002) *National Learner Survey www.lsc.gov. uk/news_docs/Learner-Satisfaction.pdf* Accessed on-line November 2002.

Leathwood, C. (2000) 'Happy families? Pedagogy, management and parental discourses of control in the corporatised further education college', *Journal of Further and Higher Education*, 24 (2), pp. 163–82.

Lifelong Learning UK (2005) *National Occupational Standards for Leadership and Management in the Post-compulsory Learning and Skills Sector*, Lifelong Learning UK.

Longhurst, R. J. (1996) 'Education as commodity: the political economy of the New Further Education', *Journal of Further and Higher Education*, 20 (2), pp. 49–66.

Lumby, J. (1997) 'Developing managers in Further Education Part 1: the extent of the task', *Journal of Further and Higher Education*, 21 (3), pp. 344–54.

Lumby, J. (2001) *Managing Further Education Colleges: Learning enterprise*, London: Paul Chapman.

Lumby, J. and Tomlinson, H. (2000) 'Principals speaking: Managerialism and leadership in further education', *Research in Post-compulsory Education*, 5 (2), pp. 139–51.

Mintzberg, H. (1990) 'The manager's job: folklore and fact', *Harvard Business Review*, March–April 163–76 (originally published 1975).

Ogawa, R. T. and Bossert, S. T. (1997) 'Leadership as an organizational quality', in M. Crawford, L. Kydd, and C. Riches (eds) *Leadership and Teams in Educational Management*, Buckingham: Open University Press.

Powell, L. (2001) ' "It all goes wrong in the middle." A reassessment of the influence of college structures on middle managers', in C. Horsfall (ed.) *Leadership Issues: Raising Achievement*, London: Learning and Skills Development Agency.

Pritchard, C. (2000) *Making Managers in Universities and Colleges*, Buckingham: Society for Research into Higher Education/Open University Press.

Quinley, J. W., Baker, G. A. III and Gillett-Karam, R. (1995) 'The use of influence tactics among midlevel managers in the community college', *Journal of Applied Research in the Community College*, 3 (1), pp. 5–22.

Randle, K. and Brady, N. (1997) 'Further education and the new managerialism', *Journal of Further and Higher Education*, 21 (2), pp. 229–39.

Sawbridge, S. (2001) 'Leadership in further education: A summary report from a review of the literature', in C. Horsfall (ed.) *Leadership Issues: Raising Achievement*, London: Learning and Skills Development Agency.

Schneider, M. (2002) 'A stakeholder model of organizational leadership', *Organization Science*, 13 (2), pp. 209–20

Scott, P. (1989) 'Accountability, responsiveness and responsibility', in R. Glatter (ed.) *Educational institutions and their environments: Managing the boundaries*, Buckingham: Open University Press.

Simkins, T. (2000) 'Education reform and managerialism: comparing the experience of schools and colleges', *Journal of Education Policy*, 15 (3), pp. 317–32.

Simkins, T. and Lumby, J. (2002) 'Cultural transformation in further education? Mapping the debate', *Research in Post-compulsory Education*, 7 (1), pp. 9–25.

Smith, R. E. (1996) 'The role of the head of department in new British universities', unpublished EdD thesis, University of Leicester.

Smith, R. E. (2002) 'The role of the university head of department', *Educational Management and Administration*, 30 (3), pp. 293–312.

Tranter, S. (2000) 'First among equals – is this possible?' *Croner: School Leadership*, 13, pp. 22–5.

Turner, C. and Bolam, R. (1998) 'Analysing the role of the subject head of department in secondary schools in England and Wales: Towards a theoretical framework', *School Leadership and Management*, 18 (3), pp. 373–88.

Index

An 'f.' after a page number indicates the inclusion of a figure.